Courage: Stories of Darkness to Light

Edited by Samantha Houghton

Courage: Stories of Darkness to Light
ISBN: 978-1-9161700-0-1

First published in Great Britain
in 2019 through Amazon self-publishing
service Kindle Direct Publishing

Produced by samanthahoughton.co.uk

Contributing Authors

Ruby Fastings

Swati Braganza

Sara Fernandes

Liz Rotherham

Elizabeth Moldovan

John Clarke

Raj Seehra

Alan Watts

Bobi Radke

Natalie Roberts

Suzanne G Lambregts

Dedication

To all of those in their darkness, please trust that your light is ahead

Acknowledgements

To the eleven inspiring authors that came forward to kindly and bravely share their stories for this book: Suzanne, Swati, John, Liz, Sara, Elizabeth, Alan, Natalie, Raj, Bobi and Ruby. Without you there would be no book.

To the Samaritans – huge gratitude to all of the incredible work that you provide for those in despair.

When life is difficult, Samaritans are here – day or night, 365 days a year. You can call them free on 116 123 or email them at jo@samaritans.org. Whoever you are and whatever you're facing, they won't judge you or tell you what to do. They're here to listen so you don't have to face it alone.

As we have author contributions outside of the UK, in Australia and Canada we wanted to include these national helplines in our book also:

Australia Samaritans 24/7 Anonymous Crisis Support 135 247

Canada is Crisis Centre 1800 – Suicide (1-800-784-2433)

To the local companies that sponsored this book to help us spread our message further:

Jane Wildbore of http://leicestershirecounselling.co.uk/

Anna Jenkin of puravidaliving.co.uk

www.dalys.co.uk

Contents

Foreword

Two years ago, I decided to write my life story after being inspired by other people's true stories for decades. One thing I realised is that although I had come a long way in my own healing from childhood traumas and attached problems, I was still riddled with stubborn and insidious shame - which kept me a prisoner on some levels in my life. I was held back continually by what others thought of me and allowed judgements to cloud my own happiness.

I published The Invisible Girl: A Secret Life, out of a desire to lift this shame for once and for all and to reach out and comfort others in their darkness, to share that finding your light is possible after years of feeling hopeless and to help other souls feel understood and not as alone in the world.

What happened following my book was quite astonishing and my life path became clear and I have come to a place of alignment. I believe passionately in the power of telling and sharing your story and now my life is dedicated to helping others achieve this for themselves.

This actual book was inspired by two people I know, one very close to me, in their struggles with their mental health over the last few months. Feeling disempowered, I wanted to find a way to help and this project idea was born.

I have chosen the Samaritans to be the recipient of all of our book sales as they helped me as a distraught teenager, when there was no-one else who heard me and to support the incredible work that they do.

Let me introduce you to Courage: Stories of Darkness to Light - eleven individual true stories of eleven brave people sharing their unique struggles with their own mental health battles and of what helped each of them to come through their tunnel of darkness to shine as brightly as they do today.

Samantha Houghton

www.samanthahoughton.co.uk

Courage: Stories of Darkness to Light Facebook Page
https://bit.ly/2NsZfhm

Natalie's Story

The best way I can describe what happened to me in my relationship is a slow and silent extinguishing of my soul. At one point during my recovery, Pete asked me 'what happened to your sparkling eyes?' Over the years, the essence of me dissolved. I used to be a vibrant, sociable and spontaneous woman and she disappeared.

The last five years have been the hardest of my life since my husband, Pete, discovered he has Asperger's Syndrome plus Alexithymia. I subsequently discovered I was experiencing a related reactive disorder known as Cassandra Syndrome, a collection of symptoms that can develop from persistent lack of emotional reciprocity, repetitive psychological stress, fixed thinking/behaviour and social isolation. It manifests as deteriorating mental, emotional, social and physical wellbeing, unconsciously taking on the traits of Asperger's, self-doubt and a distorted sense of self. Living with Asperger's as a spouse is really difficult to describe to people – the words never seem to portray sufficiently the reality of it. Partly, because it's many small things that on their own, when you say them, don't sound like much and also because the person everyone else knows isn't the person you know at home. Another reason we hide is because once we know about Asperger's, it's not our secret to share and many diagnosed late don't want to be 'out', so their partner has to hide that part of them too. Knowledge, understanding and helpful support from GPs and professionals for the specific circumstances and impact of our neurodiverse relationships is difficult to find.

Let's go back to 2014 when I'd been married for 15 years.

The elephant in the room

'What have you got to complain about?' my inner voice chides, when cyclical unhappiness surfaces. Looking back, I can see that about every five years I've felt in crisis. I pick myself up, try harder and carry on. My husband's, 'you've got everything you need', reverbs as I attempt to make the case again for more time together and more connection.

I thought knowing it was Asperger's would make it better. I've been reading books on Asperger's and relationships for six months to find the answers. There's no magic wand. This isn't going to change. Asperger's is here to stay along with its, 'different way of perceiving, thinking, learning and relating', to pretty much everything (Tony Attwood). I've tried to like it but it totally sucks right now.

When I return from being out one day and Pete approaches me for a hug I ask,

'Are you hugging me because you want a hug or because you know that's what you're supposed to do when I get back?'

'I don't think you want to know the answer to that question.'

The devastating part is that you can't unknow this stuff. Pete always said asking questions would open a can of worms that you can't put back inside. He never wanted to do it because he was scared it would change him... it was me who was convinced whatever we'd find would be useful and we'd be better for it. How wrong could I have been?

23 December 2014

I don't know if writing this is brave, foolish or just honest. Lately I've had some of my clearest thoughts in the dark of night, but in the cold night of day, you put on the mantle of daily life and try to forget what you thought. If I finish this before the sun comes up perhaps I'll be brave enough to share it. I think I owe it to myself. Who's the real me right now? Writing it down makes it real. I haven't really said it aloud yet. I feel a fraud. I have a Christmas jumper with 'magic and sparkle'. It's one time of the year you know how you're supposed to feel. But I'm just not feeling very merry this Christmas. This year we discovered the elephant in the room. Pete has Asperger's. Its camouflage has been so good we've missed it all along. It's not the kind of thing you can tell people very easily. No one is ill, there's nothing different to see. Two weeks of holiday lay ahead and I have no idea how to pull the magic Christmas out of the bag.

11 January 2015

Five years since I wrote in this journal. I've not written for a long time about us but I think I need to, to keep things straight in my head.
Now we know why we're so different. We know what causes Pete's anxiety, focus, withdrawal. He doesn't see or feel things the same as I do. I've realised how bad things were for me. In many ways I have a wonderful life, but my needs have been pushed to one side.
The boundaries of a healthy relationship have

3

*been trampled on and I need to work on that. I
didn't even know! What on earth have I taught
my daughters about relationship?
It's down to me to take control – I have to redis-
cover me.
It's clearer to me that Pete really doesn't see or
account for my thoughts and feelings – I'll have
to take responsibility for those myself. Decisions.*

1.   *I have to change. Pete won't.*

2.   *No expectations.*

3.   *Meet my needs.*

*Some reminders so if the going gets tough I
remember why I have to find another way:*

*   *Rushing home to get to bed with Pete by
       10.30pm*

*   *No housework when Pete's home*

*   *Sit a particular way and feel lonely there
       even though we're sat right next to each
       other*

*   *Be a good housewife and never feeling
       good enough*

*   *Not socialising much because I tried not
       to need it, like Pete, but I've slowly died
       inside*

*   *Justifying where I'm going and when*

*   *Endless hours spent on special interests
       and no time for us*

*   *Letting girls have PJ days difficult because
       Pete confused by it*

*   *Fitting in with Pete's fixed routines and
       ways of doing things*

*   *Conversations cut short*

* *Emotions ignored*

* *Opinions overlooked*

* *Only wearing what Pete likes and changing several times a day to get that right*

* *Cold in bed for years, not believed and not able to make changes to resolve it*

* *Pete withdrawing for days at a time*

* *Feeling like I'm on 24/7 high alert to avert crises like running out of peas!*

* *Famine of fun, laughing, cheerfulness and spontaneity*

* *Pete not knowing what to say to the girls or what to do with them*

* *Rarely spend time together as a family and when we do it's difficult*

* *Holidays at home or away a nightmare*

* *Black and white – no grey, no maybe*

* *Repeating myself to try and be understood*

* *Wants us to share the same space but not really do or be together*

* *Feeling like I'm walking on eggshells all the time and scared to make changes*

* *Questioning my own sanity*

* *Don't know my own preferences anymore*

* *I haven't cried for more than ten years*

Grief moves in for several months and visits regularly for much longer. I'm grieving my husband, yet he sleeps beside me. I'm grieving my marriage, yet we have decisions to make. I'm grieving family life but there's still packed lunches to make and children to parent.

Lucky for me there are six stars in my darkness who have also lost their sparkle, six incredible women

I met at a workshop a few months ago, plucked from different counties and countries and pulled by the same circumstances into a new constellation. We've begun to journey together and they're keeping me sane.

Apparently the first thing we need to do is self-care. What the heck is that?

Sowing seeds of self-care

16 January 2015

Pete's in shutdown this week. We sat together watching TV at the end of the week and he said 'I haven't seen you all week and it's not felt like we're together in a week when I'm falling off a cliff'. He's often used that analogy and said he needs me to keep him from falling off.
He's lost his bearings. I help to keep his bearings. I'm an anchor point.
In being this for Pete, I've lost me. I've fallen off the cliff!
I'm working on keeping my energy cup ¾ full which one of the books recommended. Letting the harsh words go is another thing I've been working on.

Since Pete's diagnosis, I've realised that we've both been compromising way beyond ourselves to try and be who the other one needed. In doing that, I'm more unhappy and Pete's more anxious.

In other news, this self-care malarkey is brand new to me! I've unwittingly been operating on empty for years. On 'no fuel', stuff still gets done but the unwelcome side effect is feeling resentful and frustrated. Apparently, I've stopped meeting my needs in favour of meeting everybody else's – er, I thought that was being kind? I have worked out though that living with Asperger's and extreme anxiety is draining and exhausting – they empty my energy tank fast – so I need to fill my tank even more than the average person to get well again and stay well! I'm walking more and beginning to reconnect with friends. Every self-care step is so difficult. I'm not used to doing anything just for me. I feel guilty and Pete's not supportive because he was fine and now I'm, 'changing everything'. I've learnt mindfulness and find it works best for me on the move outdoors. I've started journaling again and rekindled my love for colouring and creative photography. I'm listening to more music and noticing it has a massive impact on my mood – I've made a recovery playlist. I'm noticing that I feel happier and less resentful from doing these activities.

The most significant self-care seed I've sown? Planning things to look forward to – one a month – including weekends away! When I'm away I can breathe. I relax. I laugh. I find me.

I've nailed hope in a coffin and buried her

I hadn't fallen to the bottom yet. When I was away earlier this month, I realised that I felt sick when I thought about returning home and since I've been back, I notice it every time I'm out and think about going home. I'm not me there. I've arrived in a place called Hopeless and it's a very physical experience.

11 March 2015

I'm not ok. I think I'm suffering physically from stress now and some concoction of depression and anxiety. Upset tummy, forgetting things, not sleeping well, headaches, close to tears, can't relax at home, unproductive, tired, sad, negative. I've run out of answers, I can't mend this, nothing's working now. Today it feels like I've nailed Hope in a coffin and buried her. I've contacted counsellors. I'm reducing my commitments with immediate effect.

25 March 2015

I'm sitting in the sun at my best friend's house. I needed to get away. I'd like to convert a room at home into a room for me. I've realised I need somewhere to be me, where I can relax. One day last weekend, Pete was out for a whole day – what a difference it was at home – more relaxed, spontaneous decisions about what to do, then just did them in a relaxed fashion. I was also reminding myself that his fixed views moulded me, fabricated something that isn't free. I have to find me – my needs, my preferences, my views.

Two professionals have encouraged me to start taking anti-depressants. I've read a lot about them. I've decided I want to feel and face life's emotions and pain full on, alongside some professional support and increasing my self-care. It's taken us years to get in this mess and it may take us years to unravel it and find our way out!

I'm living two questions.

Who am I?

How do I be me with you?

It's like air for me / There's a knife in me I can't get out

I've created a room at home just for me. A sofa to relax, a table to journal and create at, knick-knacks that I love, that I can change and move around as much as I like.

None of the many changes I've made in the last few months feel small. I've had to muster significant courage for every single one and I've come up against equally significant resistance from Pete to the changes I had to make to be me again. Right now he's the enemy or, at least, Asperger's is and I hate that. Change can be one of the most stressful things for someone with Asperger's and it scares the hell out of me too because I know what the fallout will be for each and every change I need to make. I'm creating circumstances that increase

Pete's anxiety. Whilst I put my world back together, Pete's is fragmenting into pieces. I've decided to wear what I like as it's been one of the biggest compromises I've made over the years. For Pete it's like, 'being boiled in oil'. It's been 47 days of hell since I started.

I hurt if I change. I hurt if I don't.

4 June 2015

I'm not sure that I can really be me with you and I'm not sure you can really be you with me. At the moment Pete feels like, 'there's a knife in me I can't get out'.

This is Pete's version of emotions – he feels and describes it very physically. I'm beginning to understand that his sensory world holds his life together. It's his primary language for reading the environment and world around him when he can't see or use emotions or words to join the dots. I'm turning that completely upside down.

However, the recovery journey has begun and I m committed to being me, even if it means more obstacles ahead.

Alongside self-care, I've begun to create healthier boundaries. The idea of disappointing someone is totally alien but you know what I'm discovering? Life is amazing when you know what boundaries you want, communicate them clearly and hold yourself to them as well, without being overly concerned about the other person's reaction. It's validating, liberating and I'm beginning to feel more in control of my life.

One of the most significant parts of myself I'm having to look at is my addiction to 'helping' and people pleasing. What's totally unexpected is that when I care for me first, I am a better person – mum, wife, friend. Every other hat I wear is better. I've also realised I'm a serial conflict avoider which has been a breeding ground for strategies of extreme flexibility and compliance.

I felt guilty going away for the weekend at first, I don't anymore. I've told Pete I need to go away every 4-6 weeks to be able to live with him which feels odd but it's part of my, 'how do I be me with you'. I'm beginning to let go of what I thought life should look like so I can live in what's actually happening but I want Pete to change too.

How can I be me with you?

As the year's gone on I'm beginning to sparkle again, and I wonder if I could possibly recover fully, totally reverse Cassandra Syndrome. Whilst I'm beginning to create a very sparkly life when I'm away and with others, it's a different picture at home.

6 October 2015

Pete feels like he's drowning in the changes I've made. Virtually no conversation as he's in withdrawal meltdown a lot of the time. At best, Pete's in the same room as me and polite. At worst, he separates himself and I feel ignored. He can only survive now. Pete loves me but he has virtually no means to relate to me. In the summer he said he doesn't recognise me at all. I'm a completely different person. For Pete life is all about fear and survival. For me it's all about love and adventure. His demands are like poison. They will kill my flowers and dry up my roots. I can't go back now.

Change is great for me, but Pete and I are more disconnected than ever. I've lived the question: 'How can I be me with you?' for months now and I'm beginning to hear an answer.

I don't want another year like the last one. It must look different for me by the end of this one. I've hit a recovery plateau. Weeks of 'radio silence' and ten days over Christmas with virtually no interaction have taken their final toll on me. I'm resuscitating myself and yet can't be fully me, recovering me, sparkly me... at home. I don't want to leave, but I'm too unhappy.

Decision time

I never imagined my marriage could be turned totally upside down. And yet, here I am, New Year's Day at 6pm, sat on the sofa next to you, about to speak the hardest truth I've ever spoken. I feel physically sick. I know, deep inside, though my heart is completely breaking right now, I must say it. I'm beginning to love myself back to life. I love you. The problem is I can't find any more ways of how to make that work together without hurting us both. You're my soul mate and the one I want to talk to about life stuff. It's decision time.

The decision is to love. The decision is to say what I feel without giving any answers or solution. The decision is to speak without blame. The decision is to listen without judgement.

1 January 2015

Tonight I spoke my truth.
"I need to speak from my heart and also in a logical way you can understand. I've tried to make things work. I've done all I can to recover but I can't sparkle here. I don't want to leave you or divorce. I love you. I won't abandon you but I need to live somewhere else. I've run out of ways to help us and be me."
Pete shocked. Won't work. He won't survive it a second time. His long-term security jeopardised. Would affect family. Can't do it. He wouldn't support me in a different house. He'd be more ill than he is. He wouldn't be able to work. No, you can't leave.

I listened and I cried. Thank you for space and time to talk. Thank you that I listened. Thank you that I didn't judge myself or how he replied. It's very hard to knowingly hurt someone and not just say what makes it go away or makes it better.

I'm prepared to stay married and be ourselves, in our own spaces.

Options from Pete 1) separate houses 2) divorce 3) have the Pete you need.

Pete said he cannot do first option since marriage equals same house.

He said, 'I can't lose you'.

2 January 2016

The morning after. Pete wanting to know what he needs to do to keep me here but will also change the finances. Meltdown. Logical and practical response. Difficult morning of tension but I didn't judge or try to fix.

This afternoon, Pete researching 'living with neurotypicals'. He found a table that shows the destructive impact of Asperger's on a neurotypical partner. He recognised himself. He began to know the effect on me and what I've been trying to survive and recover from at the same time as trying to be me.

I finally feel validated in what I've been trying to share, say and explain for the last 18 months. I agreed not to plan to leave and give Pete a chance to learn more/stop the destructive aspects.

In my heart I knew there was a better way ahead if we talked than if I imagine and plan an alternative or exit – a fait accompli. One step of the journey at a time. Pete would also, 'let me go', if that was what I decided I had to do.

Pete said his autistic mind said to change the finances, but his heart said don't.

My recovering brain said figure out how to leave

but my heart said, 'tell him how you're feeling/ where you're at'.

We're going to work together through the list Pete found, a list of 31 traits of Asperger's. Pete hoped he'd recognise himself in a few and he recognised them all. He asked me how many affected me. He hoped it would be a few – 27 out of 31, 18 badly.

Sparkle is so fragile

Since January, Pete's been working on some changes of his own. Some have stuck, some were too difficult.

13 March 2016

Sparkle is so very fragile and I had to work hard this week to find it. Listening to U2's, 'Sometimes you can't make it on your own' – I can't and I need to work hard to know who my supporters are. I can't change Pete, I can only change myself – I'm being as patient as I can, but I'm not denying my feelings either.

21 March 2016

Becoming more confident. Making my plans. May be inconvenient or difficult for others but that's ok. We're both doing the best we can, when we can, to meet each other's needs.

23 March 2016

I'm always stunned when I return to this journal and see the same cycles. When connected to Pete the disconnects are so quickly forgotten and then wham! another one. I find it so difficult when

Pete becomes unreachable. It's unpredictable and can be sudden and so deflating. I'm getting better with how I respond. It's like ignoring but I know that's not what it is. Reattaching and reaching him again isn't easy. I'd say I'm 'living with' not 'suffering from' Cassandra now... it lurks when I've not paid enough attention to my sparkle.

8 May 2016

Every month, Pete's asked if he's doing enough for me to stay. We're doing much better than we were in January. Still really tough holding on to my sparkle. Self-care isn't sufficiently integrated or automatic yet. I still forget it and flounder when Pete 'disappears'.
I've got to keep the cup full.

Sometimes, I've been in almost daily contact with the women I met at the workshop 18 months ago. They are a lifeline, an intravenous drip of constant and uplifting support that boosts confidence when any of us come up against another recovery obstacle or life throws us a curveball. In fact, we've called ourselves Sisters of Sparkle! Sally, Elizabeth, Rose, Ellie, Jane and Polly – they are the ones who totally get it without needing to explain anything and we sparkle together with total ease!

25 December 2016

Writing this entry in a hotel room in the French Alps – here with youngest daughter only. Pete's at home and older daughter is with boyfriend. An intention I set last January to be away next Christmas has been realised with a beautiful skiing adventure. My daughter loved skiing. I hiked and laughed and sang and chatted and

danced. I've relaxed in a way I don't at home.
Beautiful Christmas. This is my kind of heaven
and Pete's kind of hell! 'The middle ground is still
special', as Pete said today, but can't do it all the
time?

Here's the crazy thing! I thought we were at least
the same kind of plant, from the same section at the
garden centre. We're not. We actually need entirely
different growing conditions to thrive.

Brutal and liberating self-discovery

It's been a year since 'decision time' and I feel different.
Something has shifted and I realised today that
Acceptance has moved in. She's visited occasionally
in the past and then something else happens and she's
gone again, but it's different this time. I'm me and today
I also see that I can be me with you and I don't want
you to have to be anything other than yourself either.

17 January 2017

I'm married to an extreme introvert who is ever
'doing', is 'allergic' to people, is generally always
a little anxious, sometimes very, and for whom
each day is, 'just another day'.

Reversing and overcoming Cassandra Syndrome
has been a labour of love – a bold yet gentle re-direction
of love towards myself. Recovery road was not a pretty
meandering country lane. From all that I read, surviving
and coping seemed to be the best I could hope for if I
stayed. Despite reading copiously, I didn't read anything
suggesting I could overcome it and really thrive in my
life unless I left to find 'normal'.

Love has an abundance of unconventional ways
when we're open to seeing things differently and
seeing different things. This is brutal self-discovery. It's

totally liberating though. The way of peace isn't always peaceful, internally or externally, but the journey is worth it.

As I directed love towards myself, my love for others expanded too. As I stopped forcing myself to fit a certain mould, I couldn't ask others to either. As I started being me again, I couldn't ask anyone else to be anything other than themselves too. If there are no 'shoulds' for me, there can't be 'shoulds' for others. If I can say 'no', then so can others. It's a whole different direction to live life from. When you've loved yourself back to life, you have a heart for loving others into themselves too. No more defence mode, no more masks, no more 'fitting in'.

After 'decision time', Pete and I lived a space between stories that created the emptiness into which a new story could arrive. We lived two years there.

What are the conditions for living between stories when you're two very different plants who need very different growing conditions to thrive?

Between stories has no timescales and it's ok to not know. In time, we retired judgement and control, in all their obvious and subtle forms. We lived questions slowly and compassionately until answers we could both live with presented themselves and then lived bravely into those.

New healthy habits and thoughts that cultivate self-worth, happiness and love, combined with a sustaining rhythm of self-care and both of us doing the best we can to minimise the potentially destructive aspects of our own personalities on each other signal to me that Cassandra Syndrome is now part of my past.

When I hear the faint whispers of boredom, monotony, irritation... it's a sign that my sparkle needs a top up and that's totally in my control these days!

7 May 2018

A miracle of a day at the beach together. I never thought I'd be bringing Pete to this place I love, where I sparkle so easily. On the way back:
Pete: 'If we're home in time, I'll go for a cycle.'
Natalie: 'If we're home in time, I'll not go for a cycle.'
Pete: 'Will you relax outside and do some dreaming?'

What a reply!! Like angel voices – such a difference from the comments and judgements I used to get if I suggested doing something 'unproductive'. It feels like separate circles of a Venn diagram I drew years ago, to show Pete what our relationship felt like, are moving towards each other and finding a healthy version of overlap.

Recognise yourself? I hope my story can shine a light on your dark path. Trust that with small and courageous steps you can relight the barely glowing embers of your soul that wants desperately to shine... therein lies your happiness... it's time to be YOU again!

When I renewed my marriage vows with Pete in 2013, to celebrate our fifteenth wedding anniversary, I could never have imagined the five years ahead of us. Neither can I now. Who knows what's ahead. What I do know is that I have powerful, healthy and happy ways to live there, no matter what happens.

A few words from Natalie's husband, Pete:

I now understand that I provide insufficient information in situations that have emotional content and this has the potential to be damaging to Natalie, and was for years until I understood the Asperger's characteristics. It was never because I didn't care. I loved her to the end of the world but I couldn't get it out of my body properly.

Natalie working on herself, validating herself and meeting her needs in the way she did, communicating it to me with sensitivity, respect and care had the knock-on effect of validating me too, and our differences.

I've modified my life to avoid potentially destructive communication and I'm less threatened because Natalie's happier.

We're stronger together. We don't always understand each other and we've found you can be fantastic together without that.

A few words from Tony Attwood, Clinical Psychologist and Author:

The journey through life with someone who has undiagnosed Asperger's Syndrome can be a lonely journey without a map. Natalie's story describes how to achieve a sense of self-direction and to eventually share the journey together.

Natalie now uses her skills and experience to assist others who find themselves inside the same unexpected journey. She is an award-winning and IAPC&M accredited Master Coach and Mentor working with individuals and couples, affected by autism and Asperger's, to turn their problematic relationships back into precious ones. To find out more visit her website at www.natalieroberts.com

Follow Natalie at:

www.facebook.com/theaspergersrelationshipcoach

www.instagram.com/theaspergersrelationshipcoach

www.linkedin.com/in/theaspergersrelationshipcoach

Bobi's Story

Wisdom: The Path Out of Darkness

Were we created to suffer?

Were we meant to Struggle?

Did the Universe curse us?

Did God give us mental illness, disease, sickness and poverty to teach us lessons?

Don't you hear more and more people getting sick these days? And mental illness seems to be a pandemic across the globe. By the age of 40, about 50% of the population will have, or have had a mental illness. Something is going on, wouldn't you agree?

Are we really insignificant and powerless in our life?

Do we have zero control over what happens to us and our life circumstances?

I started pondering these questions and was putting my awareness on finding a greater understanding of how this world works.

What I came to realise was chaos, pain and struggle. The uncertainty of the world was rapidly changing fast. We just have to turn on the television or hop on social media to hear about a war on something. Old patterns within our governments, financial and healthcare systems are falling away. Why is that?

It was clear it was to spread fear. I believe it's happening for humanity, to figure out how to solve problems differently and evolve in consciousness.

This is my story.

I've been known to be called the "WooWoo" girl from time to time. Better known as Bobi. I like to follow signs and synchronicity like they are connecting the dots to a greater perspective on life. I had random jobs for many years, until I no longer wanted to work for someone else's dream. I worked for myself designing weddings and events for 18 years. I consider myself spiritual, not a religious person, an eternal optimist, stubborn, a deep thinker, creative and a very curious person. Research and knowledge for truth has been my obsession!

Most of my life, I have resonated with a core belief and have lived with the understanding that we create our own reality. I've studied everything on law of attraction and conceptually believe that we live in three worlds – thoughts, feelings and emotion, or outer, middle and inner kingdoms.

I'd come to the conclusion, through the teachings of Dr Joe Dispenza, as he says, "if you can't control your mind, everything and everyone else will". I use this as I navigate through my life for answers.

It was 2018, somewhere in the month of September, that I learned I had PTSD and chronic emotional pain body. My body was stuck in fight or flight mode, a feeling of not being able to move forward and the early signs of psychosis. My body was trying to balance itself, but there were blockages. I needed to get my body in a state of peace for any transformation or healing to take place.

That much I knew. I was suffering from the inside and it was manifesting in my physical body.

Reflecting back now, what I needed to learn was to get control of my mind. I had lost the feeling of joy, enthusiasm and a sense of purpose. I was in a dark place and I didn't know how to get out.

I hope to inspire and offer you a different viewpoint to escape your darkness if you are going through what seems like hell. Sharing what I've learned, and perhaps it can help you too? If you have played small in the game of life, became a people pleaser to survive, only to realise you lost you. You are not alone. There is a way back to the true you and ways to access new life skills.

The world is changing fast, we need to keep up! 40 years ago...

I grew up in the 80s, a small-town girl with big dreams from a town called Pitt Meadows, just outside of Vancouver, British Columbia, Canada. I come from a humble home, where it was common to hear, "if you don't have anything nice to say, don't say anything at all." Which is code for, "don't say anything unless it's something agreeable." AKA, "don't stir the pot!" Just a mild form of dysfunction for a highly sensitive girl like me. I learned to keep my thoughts inside, as it might not be the popular opinion.

My parents were married in 1967, still in love today, which says a lot these days. I was raised, middle class, at a time when technology was in the infant stage. We received our news from television and the newspapers. We had our adventures outside in nature, riding bikes and daily trips to the store where you could buy 1 cent candy still, wearing seat belts wasn't mandatory and smoking anywhere was considered normal. We had telephones with cords attached to the wall. If we wanted to talk to our friends, we dialled and they answered, without checking to see who was calling first. We hung out with the neighborhood kids until the street lights came on and would run to greet the ice cream truck...

that was our dopamine fix for the day. Maybe, you can relate?

When I was 16, my friend lost her dad to suicide. That impacted me. To this day we are still close friends. Then when I was 34, I lost my dear friend, Jamie, the same way. It profoundly changed me and how I saw the world.

The "label," mental illness stung me, I never could understand the negative stigma with it. I had wished it was re-named mental awareness, which seemed more appropriate since I believe all mental illness is a doorway between the mind and body connection.

I had a hardwiring to understand people, what makes us different and what makes us the same. But after that happened, I've been searching for answers to make sense of it all. As I aged, I saw how I would morph into identities to fit in with my surroundings and what people around me expected of me.

Every time I learned something new or something I deeply resonated with, it became my belief and that belief formed patterns of beliefs. How we view who we are, the way we think about ourselves and the way the world views us makes up parts of our identity.

Think about your life – how are you different than you were 10 years ago, or 10 days ago? Here's an example. Our taught history was based on Darwin's Theory from 1859, where we live in a world full of competition, conflicts, struggle and scarcity. His theory has been programmed deep in our subconscious, and that we are divided from birth and separate from the world around us.

Some of the discoveries I made was from studying the teachings of Gregg Braden, author of New Age Literature, who wrote about the 2012 phenomenon and became noted for his claim that the magnetic polarity of the earth was about to reverse. Braden argued that the change in the Earth's magnetic field might have effects on human DNA.

Science Today (peer-reviewed), shows a new truth. You won't learn this from mainstream news or media, seems they don't want us to know. However, our DNA is not the product of evolution alone, something else has had a hand at our DNA and we are now capable to experience parts of ourselves like, perception, deep intuition, supernatural aging and healing. This is a new awareness which can change how we identify our self, this would mean we are part of the wholeness and oneness with the universe. Why is this relevant?

Once we understand we can learn to heal those false perceptions. We can learn to choose our lives differently, our relationship with self, our friendships, careers etc. If we can tap into that part of self and receive our own healings or example – this would be a game changer.

Our self-esteem will grow, and we go from being led to feeling insignificant and powerless in our life and the world around us, to being empowered and confident in the choices we make.

This was a revelation for me and a piece to the puzzle of my understanding.

I had changed my identity throughout my life to adapt to my world. Now perhaps there was a way to supernatural human potential. This excited me. My belief was that I was a spiritual being having a human experience. This wasn't a stretch for me. I had 25 years of personal development. New knowledge about the human potential, but... My mind was looping in patterns of negativity, and it felt like I was on a hamster wheel. For some reason, my positive thinking wasn't getting me the success and the results I had once had.

The year was 2017, I'm in my mid-40s. I have one son, Pierce, a beautiful soul who was 13 at this time. Yes, I had a thing for Pierce Brosnan (007), hence the name. Giggle. My life was spiralling out of control, my relationships were suffering. I wasn't wanting to leave the house, and I spent a lot of time on the couch. I was dealing with only having my son with me week-on-week off basis, my boyfriend was struggling with his own health issues. Drama with my ex was escalating. I was communicating with lawyers years after we separated. My business was struggling. I had the burden of heavy debt. My health wasn't good, daily chronic headaches and fatigue, body aches, zero energy, stomach problems and I needed to be close to the bathroom at all times. Food was my addiction and weight was appearing faster than I could buy new clothes.

I saw my doctor, and it was going to take over a year to see a gastroenterologist, I still haven't seen one. I was lying to myself every day that everything was okay. One occasion I went to see the doctor, she wasn't there. I was referred to another one who asked me maybe two questions, wrote a prescription and I was on my way. I thought he had prescribed something for my stomach pain before I could see the specialist. At the pharmacy, the pharmacist asked if I'd taken this before, I soon learned it was an antidepressant. I was outraged. How dare they? He didn't even tell me what it was? I went in for stomach problems and he prescribed an antidepressant. WTF? That's me, stubborn.

At this time, I had no idea or thought of myself as depressed. I was seeing the doctor about my stomach pain. To each their own. But not for me. I believed treating a symptom with a drug wasn't a good solution as it was just a band aid to the core problem and if I had depression, which I didn't think I did, I would not have taken it. Yep, stubborn me again. Maybe it was the years of mindset philosophy, who knows? Believe me, I'm not judging anyone who has taken anything to help them feel better and cope with life. I'm weird that way! For me, it didn't align with my beliefs and it wasn't received well if I did express my views. I became good at not talking about what I believed in. I had no reference to what I was feeling, so I didn't know or believe I was stressed or depressed. In the framework of my understanding, I was managing my circumstances. Managing but not thriving.

I was meditating daily, practicing mindfulness, using visualization, trying new energy modalities and muscle testing – my mind was a sponge to knowledge, wisdom and understanding. I was determined to shake this negative momentum and turn my life around.

It appeared to be getting worse.

6 months later...

On a beautiful spring day for Vancouver, in June 2017, my boyfriend (Dave) and I, drove into the city, optimistic for a positive outcome to the health issue he was dealing with. In a moment, like a sharp knife to your gut, I heard the doctor speak the words, "Dave you have cancer." A part of me died that day. My heart broke.

His type of cancer is work related and from exposure to asbestos, Mesothelioma, to be exact, and there is no cure. He had one chance for surgery or he would die within months and this was going to give him more time. I had always been a positive upbeat person, but something shifted. We didn't speak much the whole way home. Sorrow and fear was in the air and I couldn't shake the dark feelings. Oh, I kept them to myself alright. I was only imagining what he was feeling. Two months later he had the surgery. Although it was successful, I was told that my boyfriend was going to die! Just when I thought my life couldn't get any worse.

Time is not guaranteed. You have to make the most of your life and work towards the things that fulfill you and make your heart happy. How do you deal with adversity or tragedy in your life? Why is this happening? Can I manage all of this? How do I move forward from this? These are questions you ask yourself.

Today, almost two years later, he is doing remarkably well. Now I'm not telling anyone how to live their life, but I'm going to give you a few ways I coped, based on my experience and without drugs.

How you react to any situation, is up to you. It's your choice. It comes down to Yes, or No. Yes, I choose to show up for my family, remain positive, show strength, enjoy every moment and day like tomorrow was promised and there was no pink elephant. All while I was still struggling with my own feelings. I decided to embrace the adversity as something to grow from, it must be for a higher good we were experiencing this illness in our life. I just had to figure out why?

I couldn't catch a break. Things weren't adding up. However, my Dave was choosing his way. More of the pessimistic perspective. I respected his decisions, but I was starting to feel unheard. Which now I understand was triggering me, and wounds that I had not healed were surfacing. I was crying a lot. What was happening was that my viewpoint wasn't being listened to, which had ramifications within me and threw me off balance. It's like you're living a cognitive dissonance, meaning you value one thing but you're doing another. I was learning to self-abandon parts of myself to become more convenient for others. For example, I valued connection, sharing dreams, truths of the world, energy healing, holistic and natural remedies... yet I wasn't able to share this with my partner. It wasn't his thing. When this happens, there is going to be a disconnect.

Later coming to the conclusion and life lesson, we are just a mirror to the people around us steering us to ourselves and reflecting back to us what's going on inside of us. What was this telling me? Pretty obvious. I needed to find the connection with myself. Self-love was in order.

He was dealing with this illness his own way and together we were trying to find our happiness in an unnatural circumstance. I'd come to sense who I was becoming, I wasn't aligning with my true higher self. I was stuck and couldn't move forward.

At the same time.

The doctors told us to start making a bucket list, we did just that. In a year we woke up in LA, Las Vegas, San Diego, Hawaii, Barcelona, Rome, Venice, Florence, Santorini, Croatia, Amsterdam and Sedona. We were trying to make the best life, with the cards we were dealt. He was in pain, taking all kinds of pills, travelling through the pain, golfing, doing what we could to take our thoughts off the uncertainty of our life. And I was still trying to wrap my head around how to find joy, plan for a future and dream again. My purpose became how to live a fulfilled life when your partner is struggling fighting cancer. This translated to me as to seek more wisdom.

I started to honor the process of signs and synchronicity that lead us to places that we not necessarily would have gone to, if we weren't forced to make memories before Dave's time ran out, that's what we were thinking about. Truth be told. Beautiful things happen in the flow. If I was inspired by a city, a historical spot, a famous artist, designer, painter, writer or philosopher, the internet was at my fingertips and researching became interesting and fun.

A spring morning in 2018, we woke in Amsterdam, a beautiful loft right on the corner facing the Dam Square. I can still smell the pancakes, they were the best pancakes I'd ever had. The perfect amount of honey with syrup. We sat outside as we people watched and enjoyed our breakfast before we ventured off. The only thing we really wanted to do was take a guided pedal bike ride and a canal boat ride to see the sights. Walking long distances wasn't on the cards with his bad hip. So we hopped on a pedal bike for the scenic tour, such a beautiful colorful city, layers of architecture which made every photo picturesque. Narrow streets, with more bikes than cars. We asked our guide if he wouldn't mind dropping us off at the place to take a canal ride. No problem, he said. He arrived right in front of the Anne Frank House/Museum and a small courtyard area with a few shops and restaurants. We had 30 minutes to wait for our canal tour, so we went wandering down this one street, we had no map, just winging it. Dave was getting a bit cold. We thought it would be smart to get a sweatshirt for the ride. We found this small corner store, with souvenirs and knick-knacks the size of closet, it was so narrow with two people and it was crowded. There were t-shirts and sweatshirts hanging on the outside wall of the store to draw in tourists. I was laser focused on the sweatshirt hoodie. This sweet plump older man with a very damaged eye approached us, we chatted briefly, told him where we were from, paid for our sweatshirt and went on our merry way. Steps away from his store, we were in a little courtyard with approx. 1 block in-between the canals.

We started walking to get out from the shade of the buildings to find us some sun. When I heard so clearly, a voice, from what looked to be a teacher standing on a box and his students were looking up at him. Loud and clear, he quoted, "I think, therefore I am," I stopped literally in my tracks, as if I could hear better if I stopped walking.

I thought to myself, "was this a sign?" I was so curious and as we got closer to where the teacher was standing, he looked at me, as if to say with a nod, yes please, stay and listen. We sat down about 5ft next to him on a bench and eavesdropped on his lecture for the next 15 minutes. The quote had me intrigued since I had recently saw that quote when I was doing some research. Then I saw him point to his left, turns out we were directly across from the house of Rene Descartes, the famous French philosopher from the 1600s. A shocking revelation for someone like me who loved history and philosophy. Right then, a white butterfly out of nowhere circled around us. How did we wander onto such significance with no map or idea of where we were going? We listened for a bit longer and then started to head to where the boat leaves. I was quietly reliving what just happened, was this another piece to my puzzle? White butterflies was a sign from the other side for me, and now I wanted to consume what I could about this French philosopher, a mathematician who had lived in Amsterdam in that very house many years ago.

I pondered the experience the whole time we were taking in the sights and smells of Amsterdam through the narrow canals. We arrived, at a different location about 1 hour later, ironically at the same courtyard area that we had just left and heard the teacher an hour earlier. I guess that it is normal to leave from one dock and return at another dock, it seemed a bit like serendipity at this point.

We started walking through the courtyard, we got about 20 feet and I could hear the sweet old man yelling for my attention. He was gesturing with his finger come, come... "I have something for you," he said. He had an inviting tone filled with eagerness, I didn't flinch. I was happy to see him again and curious. As I got closer he handed me an engraved vase with Amsterdam etched all over it with a paper bag, the kind you put postcards in. He said he liked me (huh?) and wanted to give me this to remember of our time in Amsterdam. So sweet. So surprised with such a gift from someone who we only spoke with but a few minutes, not to mention we just bought a sweatshirt from him about 1 hr earlier. We said our goodbyes and thanked him for such a kind gesture.

We walked around the town after that, with no agenda and all I could think about was – was this another piece to my puzzle and finding a solution out of the pain and struggle we were facing, with this looming illness over our heads?

That evening, I pulled the postcard out of my purse, it was a photo of Anne Frank, nothing else. I assumed it would have been a picture of some landmark or countryside, so I was intrigued by his choice. I have it in my office as a reminder of a lovely day that just felt like something profound had happened.

We didn't make it to the museum that trip in Amsterdam, but I often wonder if this sweet old man had his own stories to share. I found great wisdom in many of the quotes from Anne Frank.

Many of times, I had no idea what something meant, but it didn't deter me from my quest. I'd had a strong belief in something greater than ourselves. And an innocent childlike curiosity about how the world works. And white butterflies, seemed to show up randomly, which became my sign that loved ones and spirits were sending love.

During this time I was dealing with my own pain and unbalance. I was watching Dave, take more pills than a 90-year old man, his hip was getting worse and he needed a cane for help. Doctors didn't really have answers, I kinda felt like he was a human guinea pig and pin cushion with all the needles. He was having more symptoms/side-effects than the cancer itself and the only treatment was to give him pain killers as a symptom arose. My fears started to escalate. I could tell the battle was in my mind, but I wasn't winning. The physical and emotional toll was draining me and I sensed no spark for life.

It was the summer break of 2018 and my son was with his Dad on vacation and Dave was out of town golfing. My stomach issues appeared to get worse, I was sleeping lots, only to wake up, make coffee and spend the whole day on YouTube. I was aware that the energy on the planet was shifting, I could feel it stronger than normal. I was aware I was changing, and I was also having prophetic dreams. This day was different, I got in my truck to go get a few groceries. As I drove away, I could hear myself say, "what's the point of being here?" I was so terrified. I repeated it to make sure I heard it correctly. Then I started to weep. I knew something was really wrong with me. I figured this is what depression must feel like. I decided to go see a holistic practitioner at our local health store and seek some bio magnet therapy.

Remember my first paragraph – did God give us mental illness, sickness, disease and poverty?

It was now Sept of 2018, in a small room, in the back of a health store, a beautiful smell coming out from a diffuser on the table across from me as I lay on the table, in hopes to get answers to why I was having stomach issues and feelings of no joy or enthusiasm for life. With me, was an older woman with blonde hair, a face that had such warmth and knowing, I felt so comfortable, a feeling of home washed over me. "How did you hear about me?" she asked.

I told her I was referred by a friend, she asked who and looked puzzled as she had clearly had no idea who I was talking about. I didn't think much of it again that day. I knew she probably sees so many clients, it would be hard to remember everyone. This was yet another sign, my friend who I swore told me to go see her, had no idea of what I was talking about. Interesting – did I dream it?

Within the next 2 hours, parts of who I thought I was seemed to vanish. I was getting answers, more relief. I learned I was suffering so much inside, which could have turned into autoimmune diseases. It was manifesting and showing physical signs of Irritable Bowel Syndrome and PTSD – Post Traumatic Stress Disorder. I was holding onto core wounds that had been generational, emotions were trapped in my body, abandonment, which can be real and perceived – your body doesn't know the difference. Self-abandonment, disappointment, unworthiness and unloved were the main ones. Through a process of magnets placed throughout my body, the goal being to clear the blockages/emotions that were harming my body. The body learns to then balance itself out through the energy points in our body. She was getting answers straight from my body. Trauma stored, got me to see how healing can take place by cancelling emotions and clearing blockages. Fear is the common denominator, until peace can reside, then real transformation and breakthroughs cannot manifest. We have to heal wounds to free ourselves from patterns of cycles in relationships, families, and how we see ourselves, our identity. That was me. This was riveting to me, I went several times, for bio magnet therapy and for herbs.

Our life circumstances can be triggered through our emotions and start manifesting in physical illness, virus and disease. This was a breakthrough. I saw real potential how the average person could learn how to self-heal. I had no idea what was going to happen next. This is right around the same time I came across Matthew David Hurtado on YouTube. His teachings, beliefs and wisdom about the world and how we fit in it, alignment with my truth and core values. I was devouring his material daily, starting with reading his book Allow at least twice then Ask Until it is Given. I was feeling some relief and finding it a lot less lonely having a community that had the same mindset and beliefs. I had awoken to the trickery of Satan, i.e. darkness, the world of delusion and the false matrix tempting you to give away your power to an illusion. I discovered universal truths from both the new age revolutions and the Biblical secrets and it all was guiding me to return home to the Father, no doubt. With enough pain and struggle we can except wisdom. So I put my trust on wisdom which is the highest form of faith.

How do we learn to access parts of our highest self to activate to new attributes that will bring us healing and prosperity in all areas of our life? I wanted to know for myself. I started from the foundation principle – you're God's image and likeness and you were never engineered to be self-sufficient and independent of God's blessing. That's how I see my identity and who I am. Your blessing is already poured out. Learn how to change your state of being, meaning raise your vibration to step in your blessing, healing and prosperity.

I have accessed a connection to my higher-self/ God within and so can you. I may be in the infant stage but learning the processes to raise my vibrations and clear blockages through forgiveness is a start to a whole new bright future. Taking back our power. I can't wait to continue this journey with a greater sense of wisdom, understanding and wonder as the awakening to a world opens up and what we see is just a beautiful world in transition and humanity with upgrades. Don't let the darkness get you down, let it be a challenge to help you rise to your full potential. My purpose is clear, I'm here to help raise the mass consciousness and help heal humanity.

Wisdom was the path out of darkness. Light is here to transmute darkness.

I AM LIGHT. Namaste.

Bobi Radke

Bobi – www.bobiradke.com

Raj's Story

Part One: Chilling with the Family

"Has he had his medication?"

I turned to face the guest who was currently staying with us, dumbstruck by his egregious statement. On the other side of the room my younger brother and father were arguing as he didn't want my dad to comb his hair. His words took a moment to sink in and then I felt a cold rage as I realised that he thought my younger brother took his medications to control his behaviour. He didn't realise that they were there to support his metabolic genetic condition Cystinosis and thus made a stereotypical and callous deduction. He didn't realise that the medications were the only thing keeping my brother's health from deteriorating and allowing him the energy to actually have an argument in the first place. He didn't realise how close I was to snapping, as his ignorance and poor reasoning awoke something ruthless within me.

I remember that event and multiple more like it. The unfortunate ignorance of a populace has led to individuals believing that if a person is considered disabled then they must also lack certain mental functions. This stereotypical perception pervades our culture and society and only in recent times has seen improvement with the push forward for mental health education. This is something I have seen time and again and it frustrates me that it can cause some people to give up without even trying.

Anyway, a bit of background, my name is Raj and I have a younger brother, Eeshar, and younger sister, Avneet. Being the eldest of three siblings is a lot of work as I'm sure those elder siblings reading this can attest to. We need to demonstrate a certain respectfulness about ourselves to look out for our impressionable younger siblings. I certainly feel protective over my siblings and need to remind myself on occasion that I'm here to, 'teach them how to live life to the fullest, irrespective of their condition.' Although sometimes helping them directly is required as their bodies suffer tremendously from their condition.

Speaking of which, both my younger siblings have a rare metabolic condition called Cystinosis, so rare that it has the title of an orphan disease. For those of you with a biomedical background, it is an autosomal recessive condition and only 2000 individuals are affected worldwide. They also happen to have one of the rarest mutations too. Now as a condition, Cystinosis causes the build-up of cystine in every cell in the body. The cystine crystalises and causes cells to die. This is most prominent in the kidneys which are attempting to flush out this excess cystine and as such chronic kidney damage is a prominent feature, alongside which muscle wasting, fatigue, eye problems and increased drinking and urinating.

My younger brother was officially diagnosed at around 8 months of age and had been suffering before then. My mother had noticed that Eeshar was losing weight, he was always thirsty for water and his nappy was perpetually wet. She was worried that Eeshar was diabetic. Mother had taken Eeshar to see the doctor many times and had been sent away time and time again, until she requested a urine dipstick just to ease her mind that it was not diabetes. The nurse did the dipstick test and told my mother to immediately take Eeshar to hospital. After which Eeshar had numerous tests done on him and we were given our diagnosis. Thankfully, one of the doctors in the paediatric department had seen one patient with Cystinosis before and was able to identify the condition.

This was a scary time for the family as we were introduced to the reality of the condition and that the only treatment available would at best slow the progression of the disease. At the time, people with cystinosis would live up to their 30s, the new medication was a star of hope which we all wished would change that. Although a drug riddled with possible side effects, it was the only chance we had that Eeshar, and afterwards Avneet, would have a, 'normal,' life.

From that point onwards, our family was in and out of hospital. Usually taking an entire car full of medications with us including: those to manage the condition, those to replace the lost nutrients and minerals, and those to help reduce the side effects. In particular, Eeshar had a very poor appetite, often due to a lack of energy to actually eat or even swallow the food we fed him. It got to such an extent that he had firstly a naso-gastric tube put in and subsequently a PEG tube for feeding. I vividly remember this time as I had cottoned on that Eeshar was unwell and didn't want my little brother to be taken away from me. I had overheard my parents discussing that Eeshar would be going to have an operation to put the PEG in and I decided to try to hide him from my parents when it came to taking him for the operation. I had hidden him behind the curtains in the lounge and had told him to wait for me, that I would be back and let no one hurt him. Now being a child, I had not realised that when someone stands behind a curtain usually their feet stick out the bottom and as such my parents were well aware that Eeshar was hiding there. They sat me down and explained the situation to me, getting Eeshar out from behind the curtains. They told me that I would see Eeshar in a few days' time and that I would be staying with my aunt for that time as they needed to go to a hospital out of town for the procedure.

I understood what was happening but didn't want them to do anything that would change or would cause that little brother of mine to be... not him. After the operation had been performed my aunt got a phone call and she passed it over to me as I was scared of seeing Eeshar in such a state, scared he might have changed. My mother assertively told me to come with my aunt to the hospital and that Eeshar needed his big brother. I went with my aunt and when I saw Eeshar I knew it would be fine, sure he looked like hell and wasn't talking as much as usual but at least he had that same shine in his eyes. I found out much later that he had barely said a word after the operation till I had arrived, and I feel that is a testament to the bond Eeshar, Avi and I now share. We have had a lot of ups and downs to this point so when my little sister came along a few years later and was diagnosed with the condition, we were prepared.

Avi was born prematurely and via Caesarean section and needed to be kept in the Special Care Baby Unit (SCBU) for quite a while after birth. I remember how tiny she was and how fragile she looked. When Mum and Avi came home, there wasn't much time for Mum to recover as Eeshar still needed taking care of and little Avi needed to be introduced to her medications. I was 7 years old at the time and recognised my mother's pain. So, I decided myself, to help out wherever I could. I used to fetch things for mum so that she didn't have to walk too much as she recovered. I used to keep Eeshar occupied and taught him to be careful around mum. I used to electively bring Avneet down the stairs from her cot when she woke up, carefully bum-shuffling down the stairs one at a time. I knew I didn't have the strength or knowledge to do some of the more complex tasks like cooking or the laundry, but I focused on the things I could do to try to make things a bit easier.

As we all grew up it was clear that Avi was suffering from the condition worse than Eeshar. Her kidney function has always been lower than Eeshar's and she fatigues much quicker. We know that there is a very real possibility that she will need a kidney transplant sooner rather than later... Avneet also suffered badly from rickets and was in almost constant pain when walking. Rickets are a possible symptom of the condition due to the loss of the minerals required for healthy bone growth and there is only so much one can do to alleviate it. Even now, at the age of 18, she has difficulty walking and needs to be conscious of her steps when she gets tired.

Whilst as a family we were close and actively supporting each other, rumours and hearsay about Eeshar and Avi and their condition were being spread. Often, when asked about their condition, my mother, always used to explain it properly. The fact that it was a genetic condition, that they lose salts through their kidneys, and that they need medication to manage it. However, the general public only heard the words: disease, medication, and damaged. I remember overhearing people, on multiple occasions, say that my siblings had their condition because my parents never gave them enough water when they were young. There was one occasion where a family member came over to the house and had a go at my mother! Blaming this condition on my mum and reducing her to tears. I lament that the 8-year-old me didn't have the courage to teach them otherwise, to show them they were wrong, or even to tell them to stop. I could only help pull my mum back together after they left, dumbstruck that they couldn't understand a concept an 8-year-old could.

Due to their fatigue Eeshar and Avneet would sometimes use a wheelchair on outings to allow them rest. We would have some fun with this and pretend we were driving a race car or try to outpace each other (sound effects included). But as per usual, there was always someone giving us a funny look or shaking their head. The eyes filled with a mix of curiosity and derision. Sometimes people would come up to us and ask us what was wrong with my siblings. My parents, used to this sort of thing by now, responded with the usual layman's explanation. They have kidney damage... so tire quickly... and need a wheelchair to help with mobility.

Having seen Eeshar and Avneet with their condition since as far as I can remember it has never affected me in how I treat them. Sure enough, I look out for them more as I am aware of their physical limits, but they are very much the leaders of their lives. I had learnt patience, tolerance and acceptance from all these events and knew that my family would always be there for me. I hadn't really suffered much directly myself but was aware of the support around me if I ever was in a pinch. All of the events that occurred in my early life gave me a great foundation for what came when I left home for university.

Part Two: What to do when the Pillars Fall?

I had decided to study medicine at university after seeing the care provided by medical professionals and wanted to be able to provide that myself. Additionally, I had decided since the age of 12 that, single-handedly I would find a cure for my siblings' condition. To do this I required knowledge of medicine and genetics. I packed my bags and was dropped off at the university halls in the September. Eagerly anticipating the new knowledge I would acquire.

Unfortunately, it was from this point onwards things started to fall apart. Now I had experienced deaths in the family before but being at home and younger we were able to support each other through the bereavement process. Within the first 5 months since starting university, I had four close family deaths occur.

Of these, my Grandmother's, struck me the hardest, the first of my pillars of support had crumbled. She had been ailing for quite a while and we would always make an effort to see her when we could. She was the kindest person in the world and taught me so many things. In the month before her death she had been hospitalised and so I spent a lot of time going between university and seeing my Grandmother when I could. Over those 5 months I didn't really get the opportunity to settle in to university life. Between the funerals, meeting family and going to see my Grandmother I spent most weekends travelling. I was also busy studying and didn't really have the time to grieve.

This delayed bereavement started to affect my studies, I started to notice I was becoming more forgetful and a fog was descending over my mind. I felt that I had to keep on top of my studies and keep myself together as we had so much to deal with at the time. This led to me acting stoic in front of my family so as not to worry them and provide a façade for myself to hide behind – I was pretending that I could manage.

The impact of this began to show during my second to third year at University when my family experienced further difficulties. Shortly before my second-year exams, my Father developed life threatening issues. He had an incident in the early summer where he ended up in hospital for 3 weeks. Then, in October of my third year he had a septic event, and the family was advised to prepare for the worst. Dad was required to rest from work for a long time and had to slowly be reintroduced to his work environment. After the event he was significantly more fatigued and had lapses in his memory. Thankfully he recovered from the events, but it has taken him almost 2 years to truly recover to the strength his past-self had. After seeing another one of my pillars of support start crumble I noticed that the façade was causing me to enter a more isolated state, but as before, I tried to maintain a brave front so that I didn't add to my family's worries.

As my father was recovering and restarting work in December of my third year, my mother contracted an illness which started as nerve pains and reduced mobility, and led to her fracturing her ankle, passing out in the bathroom and being bed bound for a number of months. I went home frequently during this time and seeing my mother in this state so distant from her usual energetic-self was horrifyingly distressing for me.

My strong, kind and courageous mother was now bed-bound, weak and in tremendous pain. We had set up a bed downstairs for my Dad after his septic event 2 months prior and this was now occupied by my mother who was now incapable of climbing up the stairs. My mother and I have always been close, but there were times now where it was difficult to recognise her. I was scared about whether she would ever recover herself and be the fun-loving mum I remember. I internalised a lot of these feelings and became significantly more withdrawn and less involved with my colleagues and friends. I continued trying to focus on my studies, but had difficulty due to the brain fog getting worse. I was forgetting things I had just read, losing track of conversations for no reason, and effectively living life on autopilot.

I began to recognise the impact of these family events on my own wellbeing and ability to focus on my studies at this point. I realised that I was only causing myself more harm by bottling it up and thus took measures to try to remove the façade I had put up. This included some serious and deep chats with friends and family, actively reflecting on the events and writing down my thoughts and feelings. This made things clearer and I started to feel more comfortable being open again. Thus I entered the latter half of my third year with somewhat renewed vigour, although some aspects of the brain fog persisted. At this time, I felt as if things were improving and when the opportunity to do an intercalated degree presented itself I took it with both hands. My intercalated year started fantastically, and I felt I was recovering the aspects of myself that allowed me to get into medical school initially.

A few months into the intercalation, now November of my fourth year of study, I fell when going down the stairs to answer the door and bashed my head and neck hard against the door. I feel that this event led to the next chapter of challenges I had to face. After the fall, the GP was happy that everything was fine and advised me to do some exercises to help me resolve the newfound weakness in my left arm. However, in the coming months I started to experience migraines more and more frequently. I had suffered from migraines before, they run in the family, but they had now increased in frequency and severity. By March of my intercalated year I was having a migraine once a week and the medication prescribed by the GP did not help. I felt like a zombie during this time period and had to make a concerted effort to continue. I completed my intercalated year successfully and returned to medicine with my migraines still persisting.

I lost a lot of time on placement, and my revision was disrupted by the migraines. I had still not found a way to manage them. Under these circumstances I had been struggling with my studies and was putting in more effort to try to keep up. Due to disruptive impact of the migraines on my day to day life and studies, in December 2017 the GP prescribed me Amitriptyline and for the first time in the last few years, finally my brain fog lifted. My migraines also improved from once a week to fortnightly.

With my mind being so much clearer I was truly able to recognise the dark place I had existed in these last few years. I made the decision to make a positive change in my outlook on life. I lifted away the façade and revealed my true persona, now more comfortable and confident in myself. I reflected a lot during this time frame and with my mind being clearer I feel I developed as a person. I reflected on all sorts from the things I enjoy to what I value in this life as well as the nature of antiquated concepts such as good and evil. It was fantastic to have even a fraction of my mind free of the fog.

I was able to isolate foods which made my migraines worse and reduced or eliminated them from my diet. My cooking had to improve to manage all the new foods I was trying! I went back to societies I had previously joined and spent time at home with my family in a better way than being required to for all the events that had occurred. As the year progressed I found my mind becoming clearer and sharper and my migraines reduced to once a month. Significantly more manageable now I stopped the Amitriptyline and since have been able to manage my migraines through diet alone.

Annoyingly I found out that wheat and dairy were the main culprits for my migraines, so I can't eat conventional pizza or drink tea anymore.... What is a chap to do but find different ways to make them without those ingredients? Although there is a difference in taste I now enjoy cauliflower-base pizza with a number of topping and a sprinkle of halloumi cheese, apparently goat's milk is fine it seems.

Overall, I realised that throughout all these events it was the closeness of my family and our support for one another that helped me get through this without anything worse occurring. That connection is what I truly value now. The bond between siblings, between parent and child, between family.

Part Three: Revelations

To finish off I just want to discuss some topics that I found my own personal answers to and how they helped me in becoming actively happier with myself and my life.

The first revolves around emotions; I had spent a lot of time keeping my emotions in check so that I could keep functioning, but this ultimately led to further distress. I now realise that there is a balance to be had. Sometimes we let our emotions get ahead of us as well, and that can sometimes prevent us from achieving our dreams and ambitions. I realised that there is a time and place for everything. Action without emotion is empty and emotion without direction is chaotic. For those of you who are squeamish you might want to skip this paragraph. I witnessed an individual being struck by a train only 20 feet away from me. Their body was blasted to pieces and a chunk of torso remained further up on the platform. The wind blew and I remember the little flecks of dust felt like remnants of that person. As we were evacuated from the station, I knew that I needed to ground myself in reality before my imagination took hold of the event and spiralled my mind out of control. I phoned my mother, told her what happened, how I felt and that I would be coming home instead of going to uni. After which I approached the staff at the station and confirmed what I had actually seen and the events that had occurred, grinding my imagination's rampant attempts to a halt as the reality sank in. After speaking with the police and paramedics I knew I needed to get home before I let this fully sink in and drown in the emotional deluge to come. And that was what my new mindset allowed me to do. There was a time for action, to get myself home safely, and a time to release the emotions of the event with the purpose of grounding myself in reality. Although I still get flashes of the event every now and again and lament for the individual's death, I am not haunted by it and was able to act appropriately to get to a safe place.

Secondly, don't overthink a problem, there are many times where opportunities are presented before us and we decide that we can't do it for whatever reason. Most of the time, not always, these issues can be resolved by having confidence in your ability to solve problems and hence yourself. What I'm trying to say is we are often our own worst enemies, we like to keep ourselves safe and reduce the risks. This is sensible but when it is used to prevent your own personal growth then where is the use. The inverse is classically seen in ambitious individuals, always first to raise their hand to answer a question or ahead of the game as they have the drive to complete the task set before them. In actuality it can be much simpler, don't focus on finding the problems stopping you but instead on the solutions to fix them and hence making the most of the opportunity.

Third and finally, work out what you want to live for. This is the most important one. We often hear in movies, television and novels the common trope of, "I would die for you." Whilst inspiring our heroes to protect people in the acute and dire hour it can lead to an unhealthy lifestyle where you continually sacrifice more and more for the one you would sacrifice your life for. Hence, what do you want to live for? Do you live for your friends? Your ambitions? Your pride? Or your family?

I choose to live to enjoy the time with my family to the best possible extent. This leads me to make sure that all my actions sort out my work ahead of time, complete things to a high standard and take pride in what I do. I endeavour to make my life better so that the time I spend with my family is that much better. Instead of conversation about all that is going wrong, these things diminish and we discuss the awesome stuff we've done recently or solutions to problems we haven't been able to individually solve. By working together, we become something more and we build our lives instead of sacrificing them for the ones we care for or the dreams we aspire to.

It is known that the brighter the light, the darker the shadows. So, I say, shine so bright that the shadows are even eradicated, shine so bright that darkness becomes light and shine so bright that you make others shine too.

I would like to thank the Cystinosis Foundation UK for all the support they have given our family through the trials and tribulations we have had to face. For more information on their pursuits and research towards finding a cure please go to the Cystinosis Foundation UK websites at: www.cystinosis.org.uk

Elizabeth's Story

Mum and Dad immigrated from France to Australia, leaving behind their family, business and home. They arrived in Sydney with one bag, ten shillings and their three young children. I was born a year after that and Mum did not want another baby, this was felt throughout my life. I always felt invisible, rejected and of no value and could never understand why until a few years ago. I never ever felt comfortable in my own skin and I am writing this to help anyone who struggles with a sense of self and belonging.

After me, Mum had two more babies, my younger sisters. We lived in housing commission homes and Dad worked hard. Life went by quietly and uneventfully until one day when I was eight years old, my Dad was diagnosed with lung/throat cancer and had to leave work. At the same time my eldest brother moved out of home. Dad was in hospital often and we visited him in intensive care many times. Mum received coupons from charities, to use at the supermarket and we had very little but had each other. I was a confident child and loved school and learning. I did not understand life much and trusted everyone.

My sister in law told me when I was twelve years

old, that Dad was going to die. I remember being shocked and not truly understanding the gravity of how that would impact us all. It was very difficult witnessing Dad's struggle. He lost so much weight and at one point, when the pain must have been terrible, asked his half-sister to help him end his life. The doctors had initially given him six months to live but he was defying the odds.

My first year in high school was marred by an older girl who threatened to flush my head down the toilet for no reason. She would walk past me in the playground and call me a slut even though I never had anything to do with her. I had no idea what the word even meant. And two years after that at the age of fourteen, I was sexually abused by a paedophile called Geoff, who was known in the small community. It happened while we were away during school holidays. My brother, his wife and two small children lived on a property 8 hours drive from our home. It was mainly wheat and sheep and always very hot there. Mum had found work and Dad was too ill to have us during holidays so we stayed there for the 6 weeks. I never told anyone about it because I thought it was minor compared to what was going on with my Dad's suffering. After we returned home, I began to cut deep into my legs and wrists, carving out the initials of a boy who I liked at school. I did not understand why I was doing that, except that it gave me relief from the way my world seemed to be at the time.

Dad's moods were getting worse and he struggled with the medication he was on. It must have been very difficult for him and I began to be disrespectful because at the time, Mum would take my two older sisters out every friday night. They would get all dressed up and go dancing at the local french ball. I was not included and I would mutter under my breath and answer back. One day, he slapped me across my head and sent me to stay in the toilet for a couple of hours. It was a tiny room with just the toilet in there.

About six months later, I went to the medicine cupboard, that had Dad's medication in it, I took pills out of all the bottles and swallowed them. I fainted during a science lesson at school and was taken to hospital where they gave me medicine to make me throw up. Mum and Dad came to the hospital and I felt very bad for what I had done and had no clue to why except I did not know how to live, I felt very ashamed and could sense that my parents were embarrassed. I was released with no follow up care. My parents never showed emotion and did not ever say, "I love you" to me. It was the way they were raised and their european culture at the time. No one ever seemed happy to see me nor did anyone ever acknowledge me.

The nice memories of my childhood were when we were altogether as a family. Outings to the city and the drive in movies were nice and for our birthdays Mum always made a cake. Dad borrowed books from the library and read to pass the time that he was not in hospital. He would get angry if we were late coming out of school or if Mum's bus was late after she came home from work. It was a very hard life for them both and they did the best they could at the time.

I finished school when I turned sixteen. I had an argument with Mum and told her I hated her. This was wrong but I had been accepted to start working in a bank, so I moved out of home. I blocked out what was happening with Dad's cancer after that, and it was a new life for me. At a staff Christmas dinner, my fellow workers bought me alcohol. Everyone seemed to be enjoying the evening, so I kept drinking every glass that was put in front of me. I remember going to the toilets in the restaurant and being violently ill, then I passed out. They told me the next day that they drove me to the house I was staying at but I had no recollection of any of it. I must have blacked out.

At the bank where I worked, I met and fell in love with a man called Jack. He was twenty years old when we started dating and was my first love. Jack lived with his father and mother who were Irish immigrants, and he was the youngest of a large family. I was a virgin the first time we had sex but Jack did not believe me. He said, "I love you" and I started to cry. Jack asked me why I was so emotional and I told him that no one had ever said those words to me. I was seventeen.

My older sister moved overseas permanently and got married.

After we had been dating for a year, I fell pregnant even though I was taking the pill, in July 1978. Initially I was shocked and then I told Jack and he seemed okay with all of it, even choosing names for our baby. But three months before our baby was due to be born, I found out that he and his mother and father had sold their home and moved interstate. I never heard from him or any of his family again. This was hard to cope with and after living alone and struggling for a while, I asked Mum and Dad if I could move back home with them. Dad said yes and helped me move back two months before I was due to give birth.

I kept working full time and studying part time throughout my pregnancy and thought it was best to adopt my baby out so that he could be raised with a better chance at life than what I could offer him. After he was born, I signed the adoption papers but the agency allows people thirty days to change their minds. After I was home for a week or so I felt too sad and overwhelmed. The emptiness and loneliness was too much to bear so I called them and told them I wanted to keep my baby.

Two years after that my eldest sister moved to England permanently and got married. I was a single mum but I loved my baby son. He was a good baby and no trouble at all. One day, overwhelmed, I sat on my lounge room floor and cut up all Jack's photos of us together. I never received psychological help and just buried the pain deep down inside. Dad was very ill and Mum's time was taken up with caring for him and working but she still saw us once a month or so.

Then in July 1980 I received a phone call at 3 a.m. from my Mum, telling me that Dad had started to bleed out from his throat/mouth, he had a tube in his throat to help him breath for the last two years of his life. Mum had driven him to hospital and he died. This impacted me greatly and my world changed for the worse not long after that. A month or so after Dad's funeral, Mum had a car accident and when I walked into the hospital room I burst into tears. Both her eyes were black and blue and I thought she was going to die too. She told me that she was going to be alright, but I was shocked. I did not get a chance to grieve for my Dad because I just kept working and taking care of little James. No one helped me and I had no idea what grief even was. I just kept on going on as though nothing had happened, as though I was on automatic pilot. I had no idea how to reach out for help. I began to see doctors and they prescribed me diuretics and sleeping pills and Valium. My boyfriend of two years, James, who I was deeply in love with and had met while I was pregnant with my baby, began to travel for work. I did not understand why I found it so hard to cope with this and I began to hang out with my next door neighbour who was a prostitute. She was a single mum too and very wild. She used all sorts of drugs and I began to dabble a bit too. I also began to have one night stands and felt very empty afterwards. One morning around 5 a.m. after a party at my neighbour's home, a 'friend' of mine was asleep on the floor. I tried to wake him up so that he could leave but he pulled me down and raped me. I kept saying no, and to get off but he did not stop. Afterwards I felt nothing and just buried that deep down too.

It was around 1982 just after I turned twenty one, that I used heroin for the first time. I snorted a tiny bit at a friend's house, the size of a grain of rice, and vomited straight away. Its power frightened me and I tried it because I needed something to numb the pain in my soul. The unresolved grief I carried deep down. It was there that I met Francis, who was a drug dealer and cocaine addict. He was eight years older than me and seemed to know what he was doing. He seemed confident to me and worked at the fruit and vegetable markets as an agent. After that he would pop in to see us and without me asking, would leave ounces of hashish in my draw. I asked him what I was supposed to do with that and he said he was helping me make money and told me to sell it. I had no idea what I was doing and started smoking it regularly. It was around this time that I broke up with the love of my life, James, and began seeing Francis. I moved out of our unit in Meadowbank and onto a beautiful small island about an hour's drive north from Sydney. My dear friend from school had moved up there too, and she did not use drugs, so it seemed a good idea at the time. I was looking for a better way to bring up my son who was now three years old.

The island was stunning. No cars except a small fire truck were allowed and the air was clean and the mountains and water that surrounded it were so beautiful, like nothing I had ever seen. I tried to make it work and for eight months I travelled four hours a day to work and back but that was not sustainable. So I left work and lived off the pension but I was not able to pay my rent after that so I began to work as a prostitute at the same place my friend used to. It was disgusting and horrible and most of the time I would drink to get through the hours or smoke dope which made me feel much worse. My thinking at the time was that was all men seemed to want from me so why not get paid for it. After three months of doing this, I had an undiagnosed nervous breakdown. My thoughts became scrambled and I could not think nor could I make good decisions, I left the island and moved back to Sydney. I sent my son who was five now, to live with my brother and his family on the property out west. And I moved in with Francis. I kept working at the brothel in the city and one night, one of the girls injected me with heroin because I could not do it myself. I passed out straight away on the couch, in the foyer and stayed like that for eight hours. I took heroin because my world was spiralling and I felt like I could not cope with anything. I hated working there, I hated myself and my life and had no idea why.

After three months I missed James too much and went to pick him up and bring him back to live with us in Sydney. Francis used a lot of cocaine and would drink scotch to come down off it. I hated both so we began to snort heroin only on weekends. It seemed like we were not addicts and had a bit of control over it but that did not last long. One weekend our dealer was not available and we both fell ill with flu like symptoms. They were not too bad and our youth carried us to a certain extent. No one had a clue about what we were doing. One night I drove to score from our dealer, who had decided to stop dealing and sold us pure heroin. I snorted some and began to drive back to Francis but fell asleep at the wheel. I woke up in hospital with a broken ankle and a bruise on my temple. When the ambulance men spoke with Francis they told him to buy a lottery ticket because they thought I was dead when they arrived at the scene. The car was cut in half and two street poles were knocked down.

The year was 1985 and Francis was still dealing drugs and working and one day I went to see a local doctor and told her we were heroin users. She suggested a new government approved thing that may help us, called a "methadone program". So we went there and applied. Every day for the next twenty years we drank our daily dose of liquid poison, and it did not help us to get off heroin. No one there helped us or gave us advice ever, not once and I fell pregnant soon after and gave birth to a baby girl.

We came home one evening and the police had raided our home while we were out. They drove up the driveway behind us and with guns drawn, arrested Francis and charged him with drug dealing. For the next three years he was on parole and had to report once a week to the local police station. The court date finally arrived after he hired a lawyer who found a sympathetic judge, who gave Francis a large fine to pay. After that he must have suffered some kind of breakdown because he refused to get out of bed and go to work for six months, except to call our dealer and score heroin.

I fell pregnant again and gave birth to another baby girl and then we began to use the needle. Everything became darker after that. I felt like I was on a downward trajectory with no hope of ever being pulled back to the surface to see a sliver of light again. I was a mess and we were using every day. The needle disgusted me but there was no turning back. I had a bad taste not long after that, which is when a germ enters your bloodstream, from a dirty needle or mix. I was shivering hot and cold and my teeth were chattering even though I had quilts and blankets over me. I vomited until I was dry retching green bile and that resulted in a throbbing headache. The only thing I could do was take painkillers and try to rest while it wore off which usually took about four hours or so. Francis was no help to me at all but I loved him.

Then I fell pregnant again and Francis went crazy one night and beat my son James black and blue over the bath. He ran away from home and the police were called. He went to stay at a refuge. My sisters and Mum found out that we were using heroin around this time and took me to court to try and have James removed from my care. I gave birth to a baby boy but developed lupus from all of the stress and did not take care of myself at all. Francis lost his businesses at the markets and the liquidators took his car as well. We visited James every night and after six months he came back to live with us.

During that time we were evicted and Francis told me that he was going to wait for me in the car at the bottom of our street. He could not deal with the sheriff coming over and changing the locks, so I stayed at the house with my new born baby and our two little daughters until they came, then we walked down the street and all got in the car and left. We stayed with friends for six weeks until we found a real estate agent that would let us sign a lease again.

I cut my Mum and sisters out of my life because they lied in their affidavits about me burning James with cigarettes on his hands. The blisters he had on his hands were from riding his bike around the neighbourhood. But I kept on going, not thinking much at all, just taking care of my family the best I could. Francis would come home from work around 10 am. as he started at three in the morning. He would bring home heroin that he had scored or we would wait for the dealer to bring it. Then he would lie down to watch tv and fall asleep. We would go to the methadone clinic before it closed at 1pm. I hated taking the children there and it was good when they were at school but during the school holidays, they had to come. After they got to the age of ten we would leave them at home. I loved them all so much and started volunteering at their school. I loved taking them to school and watching them grow but knew it was not good for them to be around Francis and I. He was very unpredictable and had given me a black eye when I was eight months pregnant with our eldest daughter. So we tried to keep to ourselves and hid our heroin/methadone use. But they were very hard times. Some weekends I only had twenty dollars to buy milk and bread for our family. Apart from work for Francis, school and shopping for me, we never went out and kept to ourselves pretty much. I was scared of people finding out that we were users and lived a double life to try and protect the children. Francis was pretty quiet for the next seven years and only attacked me verbally once, after dinner, and I ran out of the house and hid in the park until 10 pm. that night. When I came back home, the children were still awake in their beds so I gave them a kiss goodnight and said the little prayer thanking God for another day. Francis was asleep.

But after two more house moves, the girls were in their teens now, he attacked them both physically and verbally and chased their two friends out of the home. He also attacked my young son and cornered him in his bedroom. There was nothing I could do. I tried to reach out for help, a few times during those years but none came. My Mum and sisters came back into our lives and I was so grateful they forgave me. They were always very kind and respectful to the children and Francis and I but I felt that he did not want them to be near me. He was very controlling and manipulative, always said sorry and I always believed him and forgave him over and over again. The heroin I used was minimal but enough to give me a false sense of reality.

Francis at one point asked my first born son to buy heroin so that he could to sell it to us when we needed some. That was very bad. James had a car and his own place by now and would take the children out for the day. They all loved each other very much and we would tell them not to tell anyone about our drug use because we would go to jail. That was very bad too. But then we were evicted again, and I fell pregnant with my fifth child. I was forty two years old and very ill. The lupus was playing up a lot because I never received any care for it and neglected myself terribly. My clothes had cigarette burns in them and I wore Francis's old t-shirts. I weighed 50kg and was a bag of bones. My teeth were all rotten and I had lost nearly all of them. My hair was falling out. I barely ate and smoked two packs of cigarettes a day. I had one shot of heroin every day and drank methadone 8ml every day. But I just kept on going. At one point the program changed their type of methadone and the top of my hands became so itchy that I would scratch them till they bled. I had made such a mess of them that my eldest daughter told me one day, "Mum you need to bandage those up". So I did. A couple of weeks later there was a sign up in the clinic saying if anyone developed rashes/itchiness to let them know. By then I did not care and had lost all trust in them. They never suggested once during all those years we attended, that we should seek rehabilitation, meetings, counselling, nothing. They just wanted our money. I was actually advised not to lower my dose of methadone while I was pregnant.

So my baby girl was born and everyone loved her. She was small but healthy and I was so grateful to God. I watched shows on tv about God and I felt that he always loved us but still had my catholic upbringing in me, trying to make myself right. It never worked, try as I may, I always failed miserably.

We were evicted again, when she was three months old. My eldest daughter turned sixteen and moved out. She had enough of us all. I felt bad and missed her terribly, we all did. A week before she left, I had come home from shopping and Francis had punched a hole in the wall avoiding her head by an inch. Poor Marjorie, she must have been terrified. I should have called the police then but I just couldn't see a way out and was scared of Francis's madness. He had pretty much convinced me that it was all my fault and any chance he got, he always talked up his family, who are nothing special I believe now. And always put down my family in a very sarcastic way. We had been together nearly twenty four years and I was getting sick and tired of being sick and tired. Things though were about to change very rapidly and radically. My world got turned upside down in 2006 when God said enough and pulled me out and away from Francis forever.

We both experienced an almighty miracle when we stopped using heroin. I took my then fourteen year old son David, to a free Christian conference that had about

2000 people attending. We still never went to church much and I had heard about it through a tv program. The lady behind me put her hand on my shoulder and prayed for me and I remember just weeping at the time. Then two weeks later, Francis and I stopped scoring from our dealer, who also stopped selling it not long after that. We did not suffer anymore desire or longing for heroin nor any withdrawals. But we were still on methadone every day and Francis announced to me that we were going to stop using that too. But that was a completely different story and the lower our doses dropped the harder the withdrawals and the worse I felt. He began to go to the pub and drink and his violent erratic outbursts were happening about twice a month. I started on anti-depressants and they helped me a lot but I still had to deal with lack of sleep and my past issues of abandonment and rejection were surfacing. Also the grief that I had never dealt with after my Dad died, was lying just below the surface. We were both still trying to stuff all of our feelings back down to numb the pain of facing up to them.

Then one day Francis beat my little daughter and left a bruise in the shape of his hand, on her lower back where her kidneys are. She was only three years old and a very well behaved child. He told me that she threw a hairbrush at him. Something inside me clicked and I decided then and there that I was not going to subject her to his madness anymore. We left three days after that and never returned. I was homeless, lost, sick, with no money, car or phone. During those three months, we stayed at a refuge, then at hotels, boarding houses with only a room. Grace and I moved about ten times during those months, and then without any form of rehab, counselling, meetings or doctors, I began my walk out of the darkness of methadone abuse and into the light of all hope. It was extremely brutal but I just kept on walking, raising my little daughter all alone in the world, and then we started attending a church.

People were very kind to us and prayed for us when they saw us. My Mum and my sisters helped us too and I am very thankful that Mum got to see me living well and clean from drugs during the last five years of her life. I believe her faith helped so much.

God basically unravelled me and I came to the understanding that for all those years I was rejecting myself, probably because I was unwanted as an unborn baby growing in my mother's womb. What followed was a huge shift, the more I kept thanking God, the more I started forgiving everyone and especially myself, the more freedom I found. It took three years for me to process all of this and I thought to myself at the time, that I have made it now and will never go back. I was completely prepared to live a nice quiet life just raising my young daughter alone and loving my family. But God had other plans. After definite confirmed signs from Him, I reluctantly began to write my autobiography. I think the fear of going public with my life was debilitating for me as I am a very private person. But people encouraged and told me that it would bring hope to people who like me, had none. People contacted me to ask if they could write a couple of pages in their own books about my life, and my video testimony has been shown around the world on Foxtel TV. After my book was published, I was invited to be on tv and an article was written about me in the local newspaper. I am on more than 10 websites and my book has been placed in Harvard University Library. People are very encouraging to me to keep me going forward with the story of how God's grace and mercy saved my life and brought hope and healing to someone who saw no way out. What God did for me, I know He will do for anyone. Please don't be afraid like I was, reach out to His Glorious Light today and see how he changes your life too.

Unfortunately Francis' story was very different to mine. After I left, he gave up methadone too but took a year longer. He made so much money but only helped minimally to support his little daughter for the first few years. The past four years he has stopped even that and developed hepatitis C, he was admitted to hospital with sepsis and had to give up drinking. So he started smoking grass again and began to use cocaine again. He went from that to meth and became homeless by choice three years ago. He has lost his mind now and barely makes sense and I do pray for him a bit now and then. I feel very sad for all his children because there was so much love there for him but he rejects us all. The police have been involved on four separate occasions too in the past twelve years, when he has attacked both physically and verbally myself, my daughters and my son.

I have donated more than 300 paperback copies and given away 400 e-books for free through amazon. My book is in correctional facilities, rehabilitation and narcotics anonymous libraries and refuges too. People message me about how much hope they have now, just from reading about what God did, not only in my life but my children's lives too. My daughter graduated from university and got married and had a baby. My eldest daughter had a baby too with her partner and they moved overseas and I have visited twice in the last two years. For thirty years I never had a holiday and now such joy has come at last. My eldest son and his wife are expecting their first baby this year and I am so thankful that I am alive and get to put a lot of love and goodness into all their lives. My youngest son and daughter live with me and are doing very well too. My life is full of joy and I am content. I finally accept myself. Please if you need time to grieve don't be like I was and just bury things deep down. Give yourself time, this life is hard and we need to take care of ourselves. You are worth it and Jesus forgives us our humanity. He understands and said He will never leave us nor forsake us. My prayer is the person who reads this and maybe feels a little lost, broken, not normal, finds healing and takes the time to reach out for help and comes to understand that no one is too far gone, God has not forgotten about you, He is very close, and will draw you near if you just believe.

I try to live a quiet life now and enjoy drawing, painting, gardening and cooking. I love cleaning too and find it therapeutic. Having never seen a counsellor or psychologist, I use these things to help me process and reflect on life and daily happenings. I love being wide awake and have accepted that I am always going feel things very deeply. I try to get out into nature and love the glory of the sky and birds and oceans, sunsets and sunrises, basically everything that money cannot buy. I try to give a hand or an encouraging word to my neighbours and people in my community. I love reading *The Word Of God* and believe that He keeps my path straight and flooded with His Light. I love encouraging stories that give people Hope because we all need it so much. Never ever give up Hope, on the other side is Truth and Goodness and that is beautiful.

Elizabeth - www.elizabethmoldovan.org

Liz's Story

The spirits were back, and they were everywhere, good and evil. Why was this happening again? Hadn't I been through enough over the last 15 years? Why again did I get this strange feeling that I could always feel when I was about to go into a psychotic episode? Everything started to become crystal clear again and my senses were alert, just like Bradley Cooper, out of the film Limitless. I felt once again, alive and that all spirits were talking to me again. I was becoming a little hyper again and had not long started a new job which was extremely exciting but very fast paced. It was stressful, but I felt like I could cope okay, or could I?

I had stayed with my best friend the last two nights as she was having serious boyfriend problems and I wanted to help her but was that at my own peril? The police had been called and her boyfriend had been arrested. I stayed with my friend to keep her company but we were both on edge as we didn't know when her fella would be released and whether he would come back. Sleep is so important to me and I had had two restless nights which raises severe alarm bells in my world...

I went to work that morning feeling like a zombie and very emotional but weirdly elated too, I remember bursting into tears in front of the Human Resources woman and telling her all about my previous mental health conditions and what had been happening. She looked totally shocked but offered to help and support. I was surprised that she didn't send me home as I was in a right state, but I headed back to work and tried to remain calm and composed which was extremely difficult considering my mind was doing somersaults again and the spirits were back. I could feel them surrounding me as if something bad was about to happen.

In the office they were talking about horror films which didn't help me, I was feeling very vulnerable and this brought back all my worst nightmares from the film I watched when I was 13. Nightmare on Elm Street, it still sends chills down my spine now. It is the most horrific film I have ever seen, and I had spent the majority of my life suffering uncontrollable nightmares because of it. My imagination is extremely vivid anyhow and my mind started racing even more.

The next thing I knew, I had grabbed one of the girls and sat her down in the kitchen and explained to her that the world was about to end but it would be okay as she would win the lottery soon. Why would I say this? I had lost my mind again and suddenly felt the evil around me. I jumped up and shouted, 'quick now we must go!' And ran out into the main office. There were about 10 people in the office all busy concentrating on their work and I bombarded into the room and I screamed out, 'all of you just shut the fuck up and listen to what I am about to say as it is extremely important! Don't you realise how lucky you are and how grateful you should be?' I was then flipping between evil and good, pointing fingers at people and saying that aliens were attacking the planet. I then shouted at this poor guy and said I fell in love with him the first time I saw him and what would he say if I asked him to marry me! Poor bloke looked completely dumbfounded - I still remember his face now, he looked shocked and terrified.

I hasten to add that he didn't say anything and I didn't even wait for the response as I had now spun into paranoid mode and thought my worst nightmare was in the room. Evil was everywhere and I slammed my body against the wall as if I was being attacked by an invisible force of repulsion. I was terror-stricken, unable to speak and grasped this girl's hair to pull her out the way, and then ran out the room and down the stairs screaming at people to run. This guy was in front of me and also started to run as I had sent him into a panic and he didn't even know why. I suppose your natural instinct kicks in and if someone screams at you to run you just do, no questions asked. I proceeded to lock the door but had no key so was acting out the motion, it was just in my imagination. I frantically started looking for my dream car outside the building which is an Audi R8, but couldn't see it, so then was desperately searching for some kind of recognisable landmark or something that looked familiar to help me. I kept running and then stopped briefly at this group of people to demonstrate my karate skills which I have never even attempted to do in my life. I turned around and a woman approached me, looking in my mind, very angry and like a bully from school (something else from a traumatic childhood). She was looking menacing at me and before I could stop myself I punched her right on the nose then ran off in a panic. What was I thinking? The trouble was, I wasn't - I had lost the plot again - the spirits were around me again, forcing me to do things I didn't want to do. I felt like my head was going to explode and the thoughts were stifling. People from the office were collating in the car park and trying to get me to calm down, but I didn't trust anyone, and I was firing out accusations left, right, and centre. I don't think they knew what on earth was going on and was definitely not something they had ever witnessed before. Suddenly the police arrived and detained me and put me in the back of the police car. The young policeman was brilliant! And he managed to calm me down within a few minutes and BANG, the realisation suddenly hit me. What on Earth had I done and why? I could see one of the girls crying from the window of the police car and she was so upset, I felt mortified and helpless. I was overcome with feelings of getting out of the car to say sorry, but it was too late, the damage had been done. There was no turning back the clock and how would I explain to her what had happened? I didn't understand it myself let alone explain to someone who I had just hit on the nose. The second police officer came to see me about 15 minutes later and explained that no-one was going to press charges. I was so relieved and grateful as heavens knows what my fate would have been. I was taken to A&E in the company of the police officer, she was so professional and spoke to me like a proper human being. By this time, I had calmed down quite considerably so was able to have a normal decent conversation. It wasn't long before I was taken into a room to be assessed by a nurse, they have to get two people to sit in the interview as I suppose you don't know the mental state of the patient and they need to protect themselves. I was asked loads of questions then left alone with my own thoughts. I kept going over and over in my mind why had this happened again? Why, oh why?

Darell arrived about an hour later and I have never felt so happy to see him, we hugged tightly and I didn't want to let him go, I was so embarrassed about what I had done and didn't know quite how to tell him. We sat and chatted for a couple of hours whilst the nurses decided my fate, all I knew is the last place I wanted to go to was the local Mental Hospital. I hated that place and it gave me serious nightmares, I had spent too many times there and I was petrified of the whole environment and what it stood for. Darell cheered me up no end and I was so thankful to have him in my life.

For what seemed like an eternity and no-one entering the room, without warning, it seemed like the whole world descended on us, we had a social worker, two psychiatrists, one mental health nurse, Darell and a trainee nurse. Cosy I thought, and here we go again...

The social worker started to pipe on about how many qualifications he had, including a master's degree in some subject which I had never heard of. I switched off straight away and thought why did he have the need to justify himself to me? He continued to convey his words and when addressing me spoke to me like I was 5 years old. This sent me from 0 to 100 in a millisecond, and I screamed, 'don't speak to me like I an idiot, I know more about my mental health condition than you will ever know!' I suddenly saw him flinch and his face switch, I knew he was not impressed at all. I then dismissed him like a ton of bricks and directed my attention to the other doctor who was sitting there with his mouth open. When he spoke, he was extremely nervous and initially started stuttering. The thing is though, when you are in a manic state your senses are heightened and for some reason you get superman hearing, it's all very bizarre. The social worker stupidly muttered something under his breath when I did this, and I heard it! Big mistake! So as quick as a flash I spun around and said, 'what the fuck did you say?'

He looked stunned, then denied it and said, 'nothing.'

This is the worst thing he could ever do as I absolutely loathe people who lie, let alone when I am in an episode. I didn't stop there, and I carried on, saying, 'I suggest you tell me what you said as I heard you mutter under your breath.' And do you know what, he then admitted he did say something – he said that I was rude!

'Well there you go, why lie?' I said thank you, that was all I asked. I think our relationship was doomed from the start and I could sense he didn't like me at all. This was the final straw and now he had no time for me.

The meeting went on for ages and they came to the conclusion that I was to go to the hospital. I went to get a quick drink with Darell and ended up losing the plot again with the nurse in charge as her breath smelt of smoke. I personally didn't think this was the environment to be smelling of smoke, she wasn't happy at all and I must admit I didn't go about it in the best of manners. From memory; I totally shouted her down in front of all her work colleagues. I had totally embarrassed her and now she didn't like me. I was building up enemies all over A&E, not great considering they had the ultimate say in my destiny.

After lengthy consultations I finally agreed to go to hospital. When I was walking down the corridor with the social worker and Darell everything seemed fine, then BANG, all of a sudden, paranoia hit me like a thunder bolt as they opened the doors into the main reception to A&E. I started to get nervy again and automatically I grabbed onto the railing and sat on the floor screaming, 'I don't want to go to that fucking dreadful place!' I began to propose anything to Darell to stop this, in my mind I thought they were taking me away to murder me, I was convinced, and was in a state of panic. I was screaming, 'HELP me! HELP me!' As I frantically tried to remain glued to the pole. Darell seemed not to hear me and neither did the social worker, it was like they had turned into robots. They pulled me up by the legs with two other guys supporting my arms, and started to carry me out. I was screaming to anybody and everybody that could hear me. Do you know what? No-one who sat in A&E turned around, it was as if time had stopped still and they had all been brain washed. I couldn't believe what was happening. It felt like I was in some sort of horror film.

I got outside and was having a major panic attack as I thought, 'this is it, they are going to kill me.' They were whispering and I couldn't hear what they were saying, so this made it worse. I was so convinced that

I screamed out as loud as I could, 'God, Jesus, please, please, help me!' All of a sudden, Darell and the social worker dropped my legs and I was being sucked back into the A&E through the doors and back to the room. I was hyper ventilating by this time and the staff were trying to get me to breathe and calm down. I have never, ever, been so petrified in my life and it took me a while to settle down. All I kept saying to the staff was, 'thank you, thank you, thank you, you have saved my life,' as I genuinely thought they had. I was so relieved.

When I eventually recovered after taking some water, I had two security guards sitting either side of me. It all felt a bit strange, and then Darell was allowed back in the room and they abruptly left. I was still a bit wary of him and wondered why he had done what had he had done. We started to have an argument and he really pushed me to breaking point, so I punched him right in the mouth! BOOM! What was wrong with me? I was never violent, but I had this hidden aggression that sparked from nowhere. He grabbed his mouth and then the door flew open and the security guards pulled Darell out of the room. I saw Darell look at me with sheer horror in his face, holding his cut lip which was pouring with blood. I was shouting, 'I am so sorry honey!' But he wasn't listening, and the staff took him away. So I was left alone again, which seemed like forever, lost in my own thoughts of sheer panic and delusion. I was so scared and didn't know what was happening to me again. It felt like I wasn't in control of my own body and someone was making me do these horrible things. I felt helpless and wanted to cry, but felt numb inside and had no tears to shed. The two security guards then re-entered the room and resumed their position either side of me. I felt safe and protected and it also helped that one of them was extremely good looking, but knew it, so I thought it would be a challenge to bring him down a peg or two. So proceeded for the next two hours or so to have banter and make the other guard laugh out loud.

It was a surreal situation as I began to become the performer and was making everybody laugh, it was all very bizarre, and staff just kept coming in and out of the room. After what seemed like ages, the social worker who didn't like me, came back in the room and said that they would have to **forcibly** take me to hospital if I was not to come quietly. In fact, his words were, 'we will strap you to a bed and wheel you out in front of everyone, do you want that?' Charming is that how you treat patients? I was adamant that I was not going anywhere so eventually they ended up restraining me and injecting me with a cocktail of drugs in order for me to get some rest and much needed sleep.

I woke in the morning in the same room, feeling all disorientated and wondered what had just happened. I had blacked out which was probably all of the drugs. A lovely ambulance woman then came in and spoke to me so kindly and nicely, I instantly warmed to her and let my guard down. She said that they were going to take me to a safe place and everything would be ok. Of-course I trusted her, so I went in the ambulance which was only a short ride, then walked through some corridors and was led into a room which had 4 walls, a window, a crash mat in the corner, a separate shower cubicle and a toilet. What on earth was this and where was I? The door slammed shut and that was it. I was left alone yet again in this cold room that had cameras in the corner and an eerie spooky feeling inside...

The spirits had calmed down a bit by then, but inside I was silently panicking. What fate was waiting for me? The door then opened and a staff member who I recognised from my previous admission to hospital came inside. I was overjoyed to see him, and he asked what I would like to eat, and that my wish was his command. I felt elated and was so pleased to see him, I managed to contain the urge to go over and hug him. You don't realise that when you are wrenched away from your family and left in isolation, you welcome any friendly face, believe me. He brought me a lovely meal and I was so hungry I devoured it within a second, I even got some dessert.

It was very short lived as he then disappeared. A different member of staff had closed the door behind him and was sitting by the window on a laptop, was making notes on my actions. Being alone with yourself and just 4 walls, you have nothing to do apart from pace around the room dealing with your own thoughts. I noticed that the staff changed every hour and did a quick handover, then were off-duty.

Sometimes the door was left open and I was allowed a chair near the door so I could speak to the staff, but it all went pear shaped when one of the staff members, a young boy, was being ultra-cocky and it started to wind me up. I had spent about 45 minutes chatting to him, and I suppose, building trust with him, then I flipped again and tried to test him. The spirits were back and were menacing. I kept telling him to pull the panic button as I was about to throw those chairs across the room. When he didn't, I did, and I chucked the chairs from one side of the room to the next. He didn't seem phased by this so I continued and said that I would punch him on the nose if he didn't pull the panic button. He responded by saying, 'you wouldn't do that, as I know you and trust you.' For some reason this made me more outraged, so instead of punching him on the nose, I punched him in the kidneys, and BANG! That was it! The alarm was sounded, and I was thrust back in the room. Now the question is – why did I do that? Why did I penalise what I had built up? Now I was back to square one, locked up in the room with staff just staring at me through the little window. I was a fool and was definitely not in my right mind...

I became to think I was an animal, a tiger of all things, and I paced round the inside of my cage and I even began to roar like one, the staff must have thought I was crazy, but do you know the reason I did it? It was to try and remain sane. I could feel myself losing the plot, and then started to jump up and down on the crash mat like an ape, banging my chest and doing all of the ape noises. I now know what animals feel like being locked up in a zoo and everyone staring at them. Believe me, it is horrendous, and you feel totally trapped. Poor animals.

Game 2, next instalment: I thought it would be funny to play a trick on another staff member as I was extremely agitated, bored and trying to occupy myself and remain level headed. I pretended I was locked in the bathroom and was signalling to the lady at the window, mouthing that I couldn't get out. She came in and when she approached me, I jumped out and blocked the exit-door so she couldn't get back out. I was goading her to press the alarm and prancing about. She immediately pressed the alarm which was totally right, the troops arrived and the door closed again. They both looked at me like I was a pile of shit on their shoe, and after making some sarcastic remarks she was left alone and then proceeded to blank me for the rest of her duration. Her behaviour was making me worse and I was getting so distressed, but she didn't care. I had obviously humiliated her and annoyed her, so now she was going to repay me by totally ignoring me. I was banging on the window, calling her all the names under the sun and my mouth was so very dry. She wouldn't even give me any water. Is this really how a patient should be treated? I was appalled and shocked and even more so when she proceeded to lie about me in handover to the next person, who I had actually created a bond with. The replacement carer looked astonished while this other women was clearly making stuff up. I noticed on the notes that she had written some bullshit down which never happened, but hey I'm the mad one right? So who was going to believe me? I felt totally betrayed and mortified. Questioning why I was doing what I was doing and also, why was I still locked in this room?

I was becoming increasingly agitated as the day/night went on and felt like I would be locked in there forever. There was no escape and I felt like the walls were drawing into me, time stood still in there, and I felt claustrophobic and nauseous. It was the worse experience I had ever encountered, to the point I started banging on the window to let me out, and began pleading with them. I kept repeating over and over again, 'HELP me, HELP me, HELP me, PLEASE someone.' The next thing I knew, Darell walked in and seeing me like this, he lost his marbles. He behaved like me earlier, from 0-100 in a millisecond, and yelled at the staff to open the door and let me out. His words were extremely explicit, and when he ran in I just crumbled to the floor. All my energy and strength had disappeared from my body and I was wailing, 'I can't do this anymore, I want it to end.' I wanted to die and Darell knew it. He cuddled me so tightly and was crying too, he said, 'you CAN do this, you are a strong person.'

All I kept saying was, 'no this is it for me, I can't, it's too much.' It was hellish, I never went into hospital feeling suicidal, but became suicidal in the room. How anyone can cope being locked up in solitary confinement for a period of time when they are sane, let alone if someone is experiencing bouts of psychosis, is beyond me, however I now knew what it was like.

Darell comforted me for ages until I managed to control my sobbing. He was adamant that he would get me out asap. I felt hopeful and knew that he would keep to his word. He spoke sternly to the staff and said for me to be let out in the fresh air. I didn't even realise that there was a space next to the room where you could have some fresh air. No-one had told me about this. It was only 12 foot square and had high brick walls so there was no chance of escape, even if you wanted to. I was extremely grateful for the fresh air, it was lovely, and the sun was on my face, which I hadn't seen for 2 days.

Darell said that they had offered a bed that was a 4 hour drive away and he refused, as I would have been even more isolated away from home and family and friends. This was the reason why I was still locked in this room as there were no local beds available anywhere. On a side point this is a real worry for any future incidents and the lack of availability.

Darell left promising me that he would sort something out. Again, I was left alone and noticed a group of staff waiting outside the room. I thought this can only mean one thing. I am going to be restrained again and injected. It's happened to me too many times before to not know what they were planning, so I lay face down on the crash mat waiting for what I knew was going to happen. Bingo! I even heard them say, 'oh look she has got herself into position.'

I was dragged from the crash mat and held on the cold floor and injected, and yes, I did feel like an animal. After they had finished I lay on the floor for a bit and just pondered what to do next. It's amazing what thoughts go through your mind when you are in captivity.

All of a sudden, I sprung up and started to dance around the place singing, as if I had completely lost the plot, but do you know what? I didn't care. I lost all my inhibitions and was showing my boobs to the staff. It was as if I had a self-destruct button that had been pushed on and off for the last 3 days.

Eventually the drugs hit and I blacked out again. The next day I was allowed to go onto the main ward with the other patients, so at least I had some human contact, although saying that, it was like World War 3. Patients were screaming at each other and running about, it was mayhem. I thought what the hell and joined in. Darell came in to visit and was trying to arrange for the doctor to meet me. I had calmed down a lot being away from the awful Section 136 room which was giving me nightmares. I spent the whole day wandering around aimlessly, I wanted and craved contact with my friends and family. When you are in hospital you feel like no-one cares and you feel abandoned, even though you are not, but it makes you feel like that. My friend Nicola came to visit me which was great and cheered me up for a small amount of time.

When bedtime was looming, I was told that I would have to go back in the dreaded Section 136 room, I was petrified, and then out of no-where this lovely girl kindly volunteered to take my place for the night as she knew and could feel how scared I was. Unfortunately, the staff would not allow this, so I was escorted back to the living nightmare where I spent the night in fear.

I was allowed out again the following day, hurrah! Freedom. And I was back on the ward. Darell had arranged for the doctor to see me and I was actually beginning to feel a bit back to my old self. The spirits had gone, and I felt a sense of hope. Darell was brilliant and so supportive. He agreed to look after me and said that being in hospital was making me worse and no good for my recovery. Darell managed to get me out, and I was so relieved I wanted to bellow from the rooftops and celebrate. The feeling is incredible to know that you have been released from a secure unit and can now do things that a lot of people take for granted. I certainly don't, and never have done since I was first sectioned in 2003.

I was trying to think back what had triggered this major relapse and episode of mania. It must have been a combination of the stressful job, spiritual encounters and extremely positive events that all happened within one month. My brain can't cope with all of this heightened activity and I have to ensure that I remain grounded and avoid any stressful situations. I continue to practice my Mindfulness and Meditation which really helps, and always take my medication. Spending time with my family and friends is great therapy and I love taking my dogs out for a walk in the fresh air. I currently complete talks in schools, NHS inductions, companies and am a MIND Media volunteer. This also really helps with my self-recovery and I ensure I practice gratitude/affirmations on a daily basis to maintain a positive mindset. I am not sure how I would react going back into that Section 136 room, but people are always saying, 'face your fears.' So perhaps one day I will build the confidence to just visit as part of an inspection, to give my feedback on what can be improved for the future. My question is still unanswered though, why do those spirits keep pestering me?

Liz - www.heads2minds.co.uk and email : lizrotherham@yahoo.co.uk

Swati's Story

When I was 10, my mum had to get married again. She didn't want to but was convinced she would need a companion and it wouldn't look good for her if she 'walked around as a single mum.' It was back in the 70s, and for most Indian families, that was their thought process. My parents had split when I was 2 months. For 10 years, we lived at my mum's dad's house, with my hero – my grandad. Life was great mostly.

I used to feel like running away sometimes – not feeling good enough to have families like my friends and cousins. My mum's life was hard, so she would off load some unkind words, like wishing I wasn't born. This was because she was told that no one would marry her because she had baggage. Baggage being me! So, I used to feel like if I wasn't here, then her life would be better.

So at first, when she married this man, it was in India. She had to go from the UK, marry him – and then had to wait a year or so until the paperwork was done so he could come to England. I really thought I would now fit into society, I will have a dad like all my cousins and friends.

The weirdest thing was to call this random guy 'dad!' I did – I was actually a really good girl and did whatever my mum told me to do. At first, I hated that I didn't see my mum enough, so I complained. And that then got me into trouble. My mum told me I was being selfish. I had to adjust. Then for some reason my mum and step dad stopped talking to my uncles and aunts. He was meant to be working but was found in the bookies! He had lied to not just my mum but to everyone, but my mum had to stick by him, even though it was arranged and of course having been married before she was told she was to blame.

The three of us all moved in together in quite a rush. Every day after school I would go see my grandad and maybe even see my uncles and aunts, but I wasn't there long as I had to go home to mums for dinner. One day I thought I would go home to see mum first. That didn't go down well. My stepdad made a comment asking me why I came home first and not to my grandads – I said I wanted to see mum as I missed her – so then off I went to Grandad's. Later my mum said it was fine but I knew it wasn't. The other thing was he didn't speak English so communication was odd at times. My mum and I would speak both Gujarati and English, but we had to speak Gujarati so he could understand us. One time I had to hide behind the sofa because his friend knocked on the door, the reason was his friend didn't know I existed. As if I was a thing to be ashamed of. I didn't understand at the time but years later when I remembered, it broke my heart.

When I was 12 years old sadly then my grandad died. It really broke my heart. So alone, like who is there to make the world fair now? He is my hero always and forever. I had the best childhood under the circumstances, he bought me a bike, a Christmas tree. I was a happy kid mostly because of my grandad. Especially as when my mum first divorced and had to come home to her dad's. Initially the plan was to give me back to my real father and my mum didn't want to, so she was told who would marry her otherwise. My mum tried to hang herself upstairs, after taking an over dose of her anti-depressants. She felt she couldn't live without me, so I was told by her. Thankfully my Aunt happened to go upstairs and stopped her. That is when the family decided to help her fight for me.

Throughout all of this, my grandad helped to not only take care of my mum but of me too. My mum worked so hard, at work and at home and keeping up with the ongoing family events. My grandad loved her so much because she had a beautiful heart despite the many struggles she experienced. The next month, my brother was born. Everyone was happy. However, we were sad that my grandad didn't get to meet him. I was so excited!

Life got a bit more streamlined. I missed all the family and my grandad. I wanted to help Mum look after my brother and help around the house and I was the happiest big sister in the world.

My teen years consisted of living in fear of my stepdad. He was so strict about every single thing. I couldn't eat a certain way. I could not ask questions because it would be classed as being cheeky even though I was only asking because I didn't know the answer, or I didn't understand. I had to help a lot with chores and that was fine as I got to hang out with my mum or I would be upstairs in my bedroom. Even if I didn't have anything to do I would say I have homework so that I would be out of the way. It was great when he wasn't in the house. Both mum and I felt so free. We would sing and dance whilst we were in the kitchen cooking.

She knew I wasn't happy but then I didn't want to hurt her feelings so I just made out I was happy. The worst part was being unable to do things I wanted.

One time my stepdad had an argument with me – he knew he was in the wrong and I had to keep my mouth shut. He knew I was really annoyed but I went upstairs to, 'do my homework.' I screamed into my pillow. I really hated him and my life. I just wanted to end it. I felt so trapped. My mum was oblivious. I hated weekends. I hated finishing school to go home – I prolonged the journey as much as possible. I went to get myself a drink in the kitchen and I had been thinking for while how can I do this. I went to the medicine cabinet and took an overdose. I just wanted to be gone. Then I was called downstairs to watch a film. During this time, I was thinking – oh my gosh, will it happen downstairs or upstairs? I started to panic but I just didn't care. I didn't want to live feeling so trapped. I just couldn't breathe. I sat there having to watch this film and my mum making out all is hunky dory. I was about 16. I started to feel sleepy. My face was my cry face and I couldn't stay awake. I said I had to go to bed and I have never fell asleep so fast. So I didn't die. I just slept for hours and hours. I thought maybe I'd die in my sleep?

With a sunken heart I woke up, I got up and carried on living this farcical. I loved going to school, I got to see my mates, be away from home.

There was a point during my teen years, he had an accident at work so couldn't work which meant he would be at home more. Me being the good girl, helped around the house and had to go and interpret for him when there were hospital appointments.

When I would hang out with mum, he would interfere. I kept out of it. Whenever we went to visit my cousins it was as a family, seeing as I wasn't allowed to go by myself. I was not allowed to talk to the males, nor sit where I couldn't be seen. There came points where I would just have to sit with the adults unless the aunt or uncle would tell me to go and sit with the kids. As soon as the visit was over he would question what I was talking about. I was this happy bubbly person, but I felt like I was being split in two and not being able to be me.

I was so sick of this. I drank bleach. I added some cordial, but tasted absolutely disgusting, and I didn't have the nerve to drink anymore – how could I get out of there?

The only thing I knew was that I had to grow up – learn to cook, then be ready for when it's time to get married. I must be well mannered and look after a house, basically be a slave more like! I thought let's hurry to get older, get married and get the hell outta there! They would threaten to tell my uncles if I didn't do something, I don't actually know why, it's not like they were thug-like gangsters, but he did build that image in my head. All those mind games.

Throughout my teenage years, my hormones and rebellious side came out and I would speak back, which got me into trouble. They couldn't understand why I was angry and I would get major back pain – as well as the stress I was always working around the house, including the decorating. Anyway, they somehow figured that I was possessed! So they took me to a witch doctor. I had no idea what it was but out of respect for them, they'd told me it was a religious person I'd be seeing, I went along with it. My mum cried in relief to know I was not possessed! I must have been a really angry teen and had valid reason for it!

When I was 16, my last year of school – all my friends would go to town on Saturdays, and on this occasion, we were going to get a leaving present for my teacher, I went but was told I had to be home in an hour. We barely just got into town and I had to come back home, it was ridiculous. I was about 10 minutes late. I told the stepdad the bus was delayed and he hit me so hard on my back and on the back of my head. I just covered my head and face, ran upstairs and was shocked but in tears. What the heck did I even do wrong? I didn't even get to get my teacher's present together with my friends. When my mum came home from work, I told her that he hit me, and she saw the bruises on my back. She told him off and told him to never touch me ever again. He was angry because I told my mum. He didn't get away with that. He was horrible. I could have easily have run away at that point but I had my mum in mind.

Did he hit me again? Yes he did, but after a long time. I mostly kept out of his way.

He was at home and had nothing better to do. I went to college after 16, and at 17, me and my friends decided to go to the cinema as it was half-term holidays. On that day I was meant to start work at a telesales company, but I hadn't told my parents that there was holiday at college because they wouldn't have let me go to the cinema!

Oh boy, if things weren't bad, he then waited for me outside of where I was supposed to go to work. I was wearing lipstick at the time, I remember walking up to the front of the place of work and wiping off my own lipstick, scared as I would get told off for that too. At the same time worried what had happened. He said he had rang the colleges in Leicester and they were all shut so where had I been and that I should go home. He ran to the bus and I followed, absolutely crapping myself. I was in tears and major panic whilst the stepdad held his chest as if to say he was in pain. He just pulled these stupid angry faces at me. As I got off the bus I ran after him, I nearly got run over but we got home. He faked his heart pains and then I got a right old telling off. To which I told the truth. And then I had to call the friend and she had to speak to my stepdad but she didn't tell the truth. We hadn't planned to get caught so hadn't created a back-up story for a minor thing like going to the cinema with friends. It just got worse after that – constantly spying on me at college.

It was not a day in which my parents would be in town, and I was walking with a male friend. I saw my step dad across the road. I told my mate to run and I did too, and my step dad followed me. I ran fast so I lost him then as I was making a phone call to a lad I was seeing, he saw me at the phone box, so I ran again and hid in a shop. Somehow I went back to college scared out of my wits! Then it was home time. I went home and there they were waiting for me. Giving me the most disappointing look and told me I was impure and asked if that was my boyfriend. I said no. They told me to pray at the mini temple we had in the house, to say that I was pure. My stepdad always said to me this line I remember it so well, 'if I see you walking or talking to a boy or have a boyfriend, I will chop you into pieces, and throw you in the bin, I don't care if I go to prison.' And of course the other line, 'I will tell your uncles,' to which he made out they would beat me up. I hated that man so much. I just wanted to leave and I couldn't. He really made it awful to live.

At college I would speak to my friends, but daren't go out for lunch. I turned 18, and it went by while all of my friends who turned 18 were having parties. I got cake and had cousins over and it was celebrated, acting like nothing was wrong. I hated keeping up with the pretence. I could not say anything to anyone, else I would be burdening them.

In January another crazy event happened, my mum had a car crash. I was going to my uncles house that day after college to organise her 40th birthday. I was thinking about all of the things to tell her how much I love her but instead I had the worst surprise. She was in intensive care for 5 days. I felt like that's it. I'm alone now – I wanted to do anything and everything to make Mum better. I prayed, fasted and everything anyone told me to do I did. 5 days later, she woke up and asked for me. She had no idea that she had just had an accident and woke up from the coma. Thank God! I felt my heart lift from being so sunken. I was told to show strength to my mum, and that she must not see me cry or crumble. I did exactly that.

Five weeks later mum came home. Everything was put into place to help her heal. She had to sleep downstairs, bathe and had a carer. Over time, she started to get a lot better, but from all of the complications of the accident, she was never the same and was not able to work again. Which was so sad, as she loved work and that was really her escape. Years after the accident, she barely saw any friends. I know she was depressed and we tried all we could to keep her happy and positive.

My first job aged 19 was at a supermarket. This helped me build my confidence. I learnt to talk more to people, I think I already had it in me, it's just that now I was allowed to. I absolutely loved this job. During working there and going to college I was a lot happier apart from the having to go home part. I called home prison. It was. In the time working there, I started University, and it was out of town. My prayers were heard. This meant I lived in student halls. However, I had to come back to prison every single weekend. I even tried to get a transfer but it didn't go down very well. I was able to work both Saturday and Sunday, then the parents would take me back to Uni.

I would have to hide any evidence of fun and partying, and every single day I would have to call. In some ways, it was quite caring and what a parent would do, but this was more in a strict kind of way. I daren't tell them we went to the cinema let alone clubbing! My first year at Uni was amazing – I did let my hair down and partied loads!

I used to have deep long chats with my flat mate. I told her about a guy I liked a lot who I worked with at my weekend job but did not have the guts to say anything.

Towards the end of the first year of Uni my house mate intervened and we arranged to chat on the phone. To cut a long story short, we spoke for 10 hours! We must have talked about anything and everything. After the call ended, I was buzzing and went to bed. The following 6 nights, we spoke intensively. A week later, I asked him out but told him about my family situation and I'd be undercover going out with him if he accepted that. I said I was torn because I really liked him, but I knew my parents wouldn't be very happy. We started to date and became an item. I was very stressed at Uni as I felt like I was doing a wrong thing having a boyfriend and not telling my parents. I just loved being with him. I was happier than I have ever felt. I did become ill because of the worry of what would happen after I finished uni. It did consume me, I ended up getting TB with severe back pain, I had bruises all over my legs and was in agony. I was advised to rest by the doctors, so I missed a chunk of Uni, then I was worried about not passing the course. I may have actually got so sad to the point of depression although that is something I refused to accept after my mum's experience. I asked for CBT which at the time I did not find useful. I didn't understand it.

I returned to Uni as I was scared to face my parents if I failed. My parents had no idea I was ill as I would go back to prison every weekend and call everyday saying everything was great. They were none the wiser. One of my teachers entered one of my projects to the British POPAI awards, I somehow how managed to get a bronze award for it and represented the Uni. I felt I was kind of a zombie throughout it but I went to pick up the award at the Barbican in London. But my parents didn't seem that impressed. I took my friend instead. There were so many contacts, I had work ready for me in London after I finished the course but there was no way my parents would agree to that.

Thankfully I passed the course. I graduated with hat and gown, my mum was so happy and I was so glad she was so pleased. That great feeling of a proud parent, and all my mums hard work of bringing me up and I did her proud. Throughout the day of the graduation ceremony I spoke to fellow students but was very conscious of speaking to males, especially as my stepdad was around. He seemed miserable. Back in Leicester we went to a restaurant to celebrate as suggested by mum, she was genuinely happy but the stepdad wasn't.

I eventually managed to speak to my mum privately and asked, what was wrong with him? She told me he didn't like what I was wearing which was a black blazer skirt suit and it showed some leg. I never in a million years thought that would be an issue! We tried to keep a brave face. We quickly had the meal and left. My little brother could sense the atmosphere but was too young and scared to dare say a thing. I was seething but had to play it cool and get out of there. Although it was a happy day it meant the end of my freedom at uni. The only consolation was that I was working with my boyfriend.

Due of the pressure of what to do next in my life I was barely able to see him. We had to sneak around. I was 23 and found a job in what I studied. I worked at the supermarket too. My mum started to tell me that it was time I started to think about getting married as they were getting proposals for me for arranged marriage! I said no, and I explained to her that, I've only just finished Uni. Of course, my heart was breaking as I was withholding information of me already being in love and wanting to be with him. I was scared and the other big reason for this is that he was not the same religion as I. I was brought up in a Hindu family, my partner was brought up as a Catholic, his family knew about me and were fine. I hardly slept and I was still being spied on. I got good at this hiding but hated it wanted to have a normal life.

I managed just about a year of this and one day, I thought enough was enough. I had been invited to two parties and thought I would be brave and ask if I could go - but only said half the truth. I had to take the risk, else it was never going to happen.

They asked me why, and nothing I said was valid to them and got told off for asking, that I was ungrateful. On the day, after speaking undercover to friends as I hid in the cupboard and whispered to them about what to do. I then spoke to a cousin who said just tell them and if anything kicks off, he would come over. I was at the bottom of the stairs, in my uniform ready to go to work. I had two bags ready in case. I was so scared, my mum was cooking at the time and I said from the front door, I was going out to work now then to the party. My mum and my stepdad couldn't believe it and said, 'Well if you are going to go out dancing like a whore then don't come back!'

So I said, 'ok then, bye.'

My mum came running towards me at the door, with a rolling pin as she was making chapatis. My step dad had an incense stick as he was taking it through the house as he was praying!

I told my mum I'd had enough and was going to work then to the birthday meal. She asked why I was doing such a bad thing and why I was being so disrespectful. She pulled my bag and broke the handle and she saw the two big bags of my clothes and asked where I was going. I said I knew they wouldn't allow me to go and I know they'd tell me to get out, so I was going to my cousins. She said I wasn't and I then called my cousin to tell him to come. My mum was shouting at him over the phone, saying to stop influencing my daughter. I told her I was sick of being a prisoner in my own home. My cousin came and we tried to talk it through but they just weren't having it but they agreed to me going to my Mum's brothers house. I was so shocked and scared at what had just happened and it was surreal. We went to my uncle's house. They were trying to find out what happened. I explained that I was not allowed to do anything but at the same time I didn't want to say too much to make my parents looks bad. They said I could stay there. I had no idea what I was going to do next. They liaised with my parents, but I didn't want to go back home. I felt free and they treated me nicely. They asked about boyfriends – I refused to say a thing at first, I only told an aunt I was seeing a guy and I was in love. She didn't judge me but said I needed to think hard what I wanted to do next. After the 3 weeks I stayed at another uncle's for 3 weeks, where I had two young cousins who asked me questions, I told them about my boyfriend but no one else knew. I then told the aunty there who suggested I should let it go and that they would find me a nice guy from the same community not related. I said no. I liked this guy and I wanted them to meet him. She said the uncles are never going to agree and that my stepdad would make my mums life hell. What was I to do?

I knew they meant well but were scared for me and my mum and how it would affect the women in the family, and the reputation. I understood the pressure but I had come this far. It was not easy to have the privacy to talk to my boyfriend and I was pretty much like a zombie. I didn't want to be a burden any more. There was a small function happening and I decided to tell my mum and take it from there. We had a chat and I felt bad as she seemed happy thinking I was going to come home. I was scared but trying to be so brave. I told her I had a boyfriend. She said she knew it. I said that was not the reason I left. I left because I had no freedom. She said I needed to tell the stepdad. So she called an uncle and aunt for back up – who were trying to convince me to think hard about the consequences. One of the aunties said that I must realise that if I do this and something happens between me and my boyfriend – that they'll never be there for me! I said it was a risk I was willing to take – they were shocked that I even had a voice. My stepdad came home and I told him. I got the angriest look. You could tell he wanted to kill me and he asked what caste he was. He said that was very bad and were more concerned how bad they'd look within the community. There was some shouting going on and putting me down. They tried to persuade me to change my mind. In the meantime I texted my boyfriend's sister to rescue me and she arrived. My uncle told her she was a family breaker, I was so surprised at this uncle that I thought highly of, he was letting me down. I honestly thought he would think that my happiness would be most important. It hurt and I was shocked at the lack of support. My stepdad shouted and fell to the floor telling me to get out and he began to rub his chest, faking a heart attack – even my poor sweet mum didn't believe it but went running to him. They all told me to get out. I said he was lying and that he always used emotional blackmail to try and make me feel bad. Me and my sister in-law went upstairs to pack the rest of my bags. My mum cried begging me not to do this, and then told me to get out. We drove away. I had no clue what the next step was. I felt like I had fell off a mountain multiple times but was still climbing.

I had just been disowned by the whole family and was scared. I stayed at my boyfriend's house the first night completely spaced out. I then stayed at my cousin's for a week then I found a room to rent near my work and away from family. I knew I had to be brave – work hard, pay the rent and get on with my life. I had all this freedom and had to pinch myself. I was able to go to the corner shop without worrying about getting permission. I could colour and cut my hair and speak to whoever I wanted. I was able to be with my boyfriend and be happy.

Now 18 years on, there were only a few times I saw my parents. There was a point we were speaking but they changed their minds. I did my best to try and make amends but every time I would get a knock back. It was hurtful, I was classed as damaged. I was lucky enough to have some good cousins still speak to me, at first it was undercover. People wanted to know the truth instead of the twisted lies that my stepdad had started. I missed my mum so much and now, just 8 weeks ago, she has passed away. It just feels sad and broken. I wished so much to have had more of a relationship with her but she chose not to. I can say I tried and gave it my best shot in all the years. People will say what they may but I know the truth and so does my mum.

I'm glad I became strong. I feel like a lot of my strength comes from my Mum's past and how she overcame so much. Despite how I was treated, I picked out the good, and used it as my strength and determination for a positive outcome. I thank everyone who supported me.

Over the past 18 years I have had to do a lot of work on myself to feel normal - whatever that is. Ultimately all I ever wanted was to be happy and free. Emotions happen, dwelling happens and so does over thinking but I'm in a way better place than ever - I'm happy and working on bettering myself and my health. I'm so glad I did what I did - I have no regrets. I am living my life to the best I can and will continue to do so.

Swati - Facebook : https://bit.ly/2X5ilo9

Sara's Story

Days blended into nights, hours felt like decades, minutes felt like weeks. I was surviving on very little food or sleep whilst my mind tried to make sense of the mess I was in. I purposely let myself go, in the hope that the more unwell I became, the less I would have to care for my daughter Aarya. Support didn't come in the forms I expected, and I was often left to fend for myself with this strange creature I didn't know or want anything to do with. Not to mention I was terrified of too. You may be thinking; how can someone feel that way about their precious new-born? It's crazy right? My journey into motherhood has been just that, worlds apart from the one I dreamt of.

Instead of feeling guilty about the memories I didn't have with Aarya, I invest energy in making a brighter future for myself and for other Mums. I truly hope that sharing my story will help people. My vision is that by reading this you'll be able to recognise warning signs of maternal mental distress and know what help to reach out for.

I also aim to empower those that don't know about the illnesses that can accompany this phase. Something I live by is the term; 'knowledge is power.' The more we know about something, the better equipped we are to deal with it. I have learned this the hard way, but you don't have to. If professionals listened to me when I was pregnant, spoke to me about risks and fed me with knowledge, I may not have gone through what I did. Hindsight is a beautiful thing wouldn't you agree?

It was July 2015, picture that cheesy, movie-like moment when someone gets a positive pregnancy test. My partner Dan and I decided we wanted to start a family. I was sure I wanted this more than anything, it was Dan who needed convincing. Needless to say, there I was, staring in awe at the blue stick! I kept checking it just to make sure. I was over the moon and couldn't wait to tell my family and friends.

Within the first few weeks of finding out I was up the duff, I lost my job. The amount of stress caused as a result of that was unfathomable, namely two house moves within 3 months and a huge amount of emotional turmoil. I don't want to dwell on this part, other than to illustrate the knock-on effect stress can have during pregnancy. Little did I know at the time, this would increase my chances of developing a mental health problem. I knew stress could harm an unborn child but didn't know that it would directly affect my mental health. How incredibly naive I was! There's so much I could have done (my good old friend hindsight strikes again).

On the whole, I was happy during pregnancy, despite the hiccup at the beginning. I was looking forward to Aarya's arrival and doing the usual nesting activities. I had a Babymoon, a Baby Shower and decorated the nursery so I was super prepared (or so I thought). On reflection, my strive to be, 'prepared,' and tendency towards perfectionism was concerning. I remember relishing in folding baby clothes and checking then re-checking my hospital bag. Family and friends have shared since that I was obsessed with being pregnant and had to do everything just so, I was very particular.

Again, I didn't realise at the time but the traits I was displaying made me 'high risk.' This was without the potential genetic risk I also incurred from my mother.

From the word go, I told my midwife that my mother had suffered with Postpartum Psychosis after the birth of my sister and distinctly remember her noting this. There was no follow up from that. I also recollect going for a routine appointment and feeling anxious. I couldn't put my finger on it but told the midwife and saw her note it down. Nothing more was said or done. When it came to the next appointment, they thought Aarya's heartbeat was irregular, I became anxious there was something wrong and it was my fault. This was recorded in my notes yet again, but no follow up. After this false alarm I calmed down to my, 'usual,' self. My, 'usual,' self, meant fantasising that my birth and the months to follow would be perfect, as I was going to be a natural with my maternal instinct. I had an idealistic vision of what motherhood looked like, not a realistic one.

Fast forward to the labour. I was convinced Aarya would arrive early as she had been in position, ready for take-off for quite some time. I had a slow early labour stage, meaning I had contractions for almost 3 days. I tried all the natural remedies to help get things moving. After our third visit to hospital we were finally admitted, I was 5cm dilated, woohoo! This was a bizarre sense of relief that she was coming but also a reminder that shit was about to get real. On paper, the rest was textbook. I sailed through active labour listening to classical music. I had no pain relief and had a water birth, just like I'd planned. My partner Dan was an absolute trooper, wiping my sweaty head with a cold towel. He didn't even tell me about the floaters until it was all over.

During the final stages of labour I had a taste of losing control of my mind. At one point I remember seeing the midwives hold Aarya and thinking it was over. I was eagerly awaiting that skin to skin contact

I had heard about. To my surprise I was still pushing at this point and was actually having an hallucination. Whether this was caused by lack of sleep, Entonox or a Psychotic episode, I'll never know. The labour was a blur to me, except when she shot across the birthing pool like an Olympic Swimmer!

Let's cut to the chase, the moment I'd longed for, holding my precious infant in my arms. When she was handed over I felt an overwhelming sense of emptiness. Rather than being filled with love and joy, I felt as if part of me had been stripped away. I guess I was right because the, 'Me,' I was before would never be the same again. I thought, 'what the hell have I done and why did I think bringing a helpless being into the world was a good idea?' It felt like a huge mistake, yet this was something I'd looked forward to my whole life.

The numb feeling soon shifted to panic when it registered that I was responsible for someone's life! Gradually this became more intense whilst I struggled to breastfeed. I had lost a lot of blood and was in pain due to a significant tear and stitches. I also hadn't slept for 3 days. Unfortunately, the midwives and other professionals caused unnecessary stress, heightening the upset I was already experiencing. I touch on this in the next paragraph. I opted to stay in hospital for the night because I was determined to breastfeed and wanted as much support as possible. I'd been clutching on to the book Breast is Best during pregnancy. Each time I struggled to get Aarya to latch on, I pressed the red button for assistance. I knew I wouldn't have this luxury at home so made the most of it. On reflection (and with my Therapist hat now firmly on), I can see that I was excessively overthinking. I was anxious about everything. Anxious about changing nappies, going home, not going home, feeding, being alone, anxious about my future and everything in it.

I ended up spending a second night in hospital due to certain things being overlooked. After delivering the placenta, midwives forgot to check it and take a sample to determine Aarya's blood type. This meant that over the next few hours, a Doctor tried no less than 5 times to take her blood. Bearing in mind she was less than 24 hours old, this was no easy task. The poor little thing was used as a pin cushion. It was shortly after, that Dan left us for a couple of hours to go and get some rest. He wasn't allowed to stay overnight in hospital. The sheer terror and panic I experienced when he left was extreme. I did not feel capable of looking after Aarya alone. I needed and wanted Dan with us at all times.

Each time I felt this overwhelm, I told a member of staff yet in my hospital notes it says; 'Mother and baby fine, mother exclusively breastfeeding.' I was discharged after the second night. Dan was excited about getting us home, I on the other hand was petrified. My hands shook as I put her in the car seat and tried to suppress my feelings. Deep down I knew I should be happy, excited and grateful. Some vital advice here for pregnant women and new mothers; don't let anyone tell you that you should feel a certain way. Try not to believe everything about the, 'fairy-tale,' media portrays of motherhood. I wish people talked more about the dark thoughts, feelings of inadequacy and the crap that comes with it. Maybe it's due to guilt, maybe it's ego, maybe it's stigma? Whatever the reason is, it's not your fault. It's natural to believe what you want and block out what you don't want to hear.

In the first two days at home I became increasingly unwell. The onset was rapid which meant I was able to recognise it and ask for help fast. It hit me like a tonne of bricks and knocked me down. Just when I thought I was getting better it would come back and knock me down a few more times, just to be sure I was well and truly screwed. Those first days were surreal, I had out of body experiences, couldn't sleep, I wouldn't even get dressed or eat. My partner was obviously worried about me as was I. I tried to dismiss intrusive thoughts and put them down to hormones or tiredness. One memory that remains is feeling detached from my body and from reality, I was in a waking nightmare, completely trapped.

I had zero motivation to tend to Aarya. I didn't want to hold her, dress her or change her. My mind was telling me I couldn't and that she needed someone else to look after her. Also, she instilled such a fear in me that I felt physically sick when she made any noises or movements. I genuinely believed that Dan and Aarya would be better off without me. He used to pick her up and bring her to me to help her latch on for a feed. Even if I was told I was doing it right, I didn't believe anything anyone said. I didn't think Aarya was getting any milk which fuelled my Anxiety and belief that I was a terrible Mum. By this point I knew something was wrong and it wasn't just, 'Baby Blues,' so asked for an urgent visit from a Midwife. Wow, she was about as helpful as a chocolate fireguard! Talk about saying the wrong thing at the wrong time. 'You just need to man up and get on with it.'

After that, I spiralled further in to an extremely desperate place that I could see no way out of. My intrusive thoughts were continuous and intense. Picture a bed-bound person trembling uncontrollably, staring at the ceiling... that was me.

I feel it's important to mention some of the symptoms I experienced so you too can be aware of what to look out for, whether you are the new Mum, Dad, Friend/Family member;

- Lack of motivation to care for baby
- Lack of self-care (Not showering or cleaning teeth etc)
- Severe low mood/mood swings
- Change in personality
- Not able to sleep
- Developing new rituals/habits

- Not wanting to talk to anyone
- Difficulty bonding with child/avoiding eye contact
- High levels of Anxiety (especially baby related)
- Thoughts of harming oneself or others (mostly the baby)
- Wanting to give the baby away/leave
- Hallucinations
- Lack of enjoyment in anything
- Extreme fatigue/trouble concentrating
- Confusion/short-term memory loss
- Loss of inhibitions
- Racing thoughts
- Loss of identity
- Writing/making lists
- Feeling suspicious of the baby/of other people
- Worrying about everything
- Seeking reassurance all the time
- Not feeling capable/lack of confidence
- Avoidance of triggers (Avoiding changing nappies etc)
- Believing one is a terrible Mum/person
- Reluctance to accept new dynamics/responsibilities

As previously mentioned, I was somehow aware of what was going on in my head so told my partner and mother, however I didn't tell them everything in fear of being locked up. I especially didn't want to disclose everything to Dan as I felt he wouldn't love me. I told my mother to hide all the knives in the house as I didn't know what I was capable of. Fear and guilt is too often what prevents people admitting they need help. Fear of failure, of being a bad parent, letting people down, being ostracised, the list is endless. If you think somebody might be struggling with a Postnatal Illness, then please make time to ask how they really are and actively listen. Particularly if they've had a traumatic

birth, history of mental illness, stressful pregnancy or
have no support network.

Quite soon after confessing I couldn't do this
anymore, this motherhood malarkey, help was called for.
I went to A&E to be seen by an out of hours doctor.
Dan bravely took me along whilst the rest of my family
who'd travelled from opposite ends of the country
mucked-in looking after Aarya.

I don't remember a lot of what happened when
I saw that Doctor except that I couldn't stop shaking.
I was totally wired and frozen in fear. A crisis team
came to see me at home later that night and gave me
a cocktail of drugs intended to calm me down and
help me get some sleep (by this point I hadn't slept in
a week). I am normally completely anti-medication but
was desperate to feel better. I'd have taken anything! I
got about 3 hours sleep, after which I was back in the
grasps of Hell. My regard for myself and other people
by now was in short supply, I was uncharacteristically
narcissistic. I didn't care that I was neglecting my baby,
I didn't mind that everyone was having to do everything
for me, I was rude and ungrateful yet so very helpless
and sorry.

On day 5 I was admitted to a women's ward in
an acute psychiatric hospital. This was the most scary
decision myself or my family have ever had to make. We
were torn because none of us felt safe. As a family, we
were advised that I needed to be in hospital. Unfortunately, there were no spare beds in a Mother and Baby
unit, anywhere in the country. This proves that the
demand for this type of care far outweighs resources. So
what were we to do? Wait until something bad happened
and I got worse? Or put me in a, 'safe,' place until a bed
became free? We chose the latter. I was able to go in as a
voluntary patient because I had not acted on my thoughts.
To some extent my rational brain was still there.

One of the hardest things was not knowing how
long I'd have to stay. It could be one day, it could be

weeks. When asked about what it was like, it's an incredibly difficult part of my story to re-live. As I am writing this I have to remind myself I am safe and ok, it's just a memory. With my mother having had such a similar experience, it was really tough not to feel the fear in her too. It brought her memories back of being in that frightening place. A meeting took place with my Mother, Dan, a Psychiatrist and someone else (I can't remember who). The fear I saw on my mother's face was enough, an unspoken language of deep understanding.

Thankfully I was only there 5 days before being transferred to a Mother and Baby unit. I spent those few days hovering by the office, checking if they'd had any news yet about me moving. I was even more frightened about being in a M&B unit because that meant being confronted with the thing I was most terrified of, Aarya. She was referred to as, 'baby,' back then as I didn't personify her, I felt no attachment. I didn't want to go however I couldn't spend a moment longer feeling like an animal in a zoo, surrounded by poorly people. I am not saying these units don't have their place, they save people's lives. For me however, being around unwell people made me worse. It planted seeds in my brain that weren't there before, ideas about suicide, and simply reinforced how ill I was. It opened my eyes to a new realm that I thought would be my reality forever. I felt that I was stuck in a room and left to rot. Staff didn't know what I was experiencing as it wasn't a specialist unit. I had just been separated from my 5-day-old and was totally alone; broken, lost, frightened, a complete failure. I was spoken to in a condescending way, as if I didn't understand anything. And the worst part was being checked on every 15 minutes. My door had a hatch so that when it was closed they could open it to check on me. Bearing in mind that I had now had about 3 hours sleep in over a week, this added to my problems. It felt like I was stuck in some twisted experiment about sleep deprivation, having a torch shone on me every 15 minutes.

The rest of my time was spent writing down all my racing thoughts, then relaying everything I'd written to my Mother and Sister. For some reason I didn't want to speak to Dan or my Father when I was there. Perhaps this was due to embarrassment about where I was and what I was going through. I had the perception that my mum would understand it all. I used to clock watch, eagerly awaiting the next visit. My mother and sister naturally wanted to tell me how Aarya was doing and show me pictures, but I was having none of it. I only wanted to talk about myself and how I was feeling. Me, myself and I!

Even though I was scared of going in to the other unit, I had a fairly positive preconception of what it would be like. My mother had been in one when she had my sister and got the care she really needed. I thought I'd be around people who knew what to do, people to help look after Aarya and be given the opportunity to rest. This was also the picture painted to me during my admission meeting. There was a glimmer of hope for the first time since the birth. I was going to get the right help and get better. Dan travelled there with Aarya because I only agreed to go if she wasn't in the same car as me. I came separately with my Mother & Sister. Naively I believed it when I was told Aarya wouldn't have to sleep in the same room as me until I felt well enough. This was such a comforting thought as she'd be in safe hands with the Nursery Nurses and I with the Psychiatric Nurses. How things changed. I know that the professionals were keen to start developing mine and Aarya's bond but at that point in time I just needed someone to look after me and allow me to rest. When you think about what your body goes through during pregnancy and labour, its huge. In some other cultures people worship new Mothers, they cook hot meals for them, bathe them and even help take care of the baby. We could learn a lot from this approach!

Almost immediately after my family left, I was reluctantly reunited with Aarya. Everything I expected went out of the window. It was now me and Aarya in a strange place, again surrounded by poorly people. As you'll come to know, I do a lot of reflecting. It helps me heal, learn about myself and the illness. I am now a trained Psychotherapist and it is clear that by taking me away from my safe place (where I had some sense of control), and away from having my loved ones around me was counterintuitive. I don't dispute any decisions my family made as we were all emotionally hijacked. It's only after the event we have come to realise that it perhaps wasn't the best place for me. Again, I am not saying these places don't help, some units are incredible, there just isn't enough consistency.

The next few weeks were characterised by sleepless nights, lack of support, avoidance behaviours, wanting it all to stop and being drugged up to the eyeballs. The only thing that kept me going every day was knowing that Dan was coming to visit us. He was my absolute rock and came every single day for almost 3 months. I was obsessed with when he was coming and how long he'd stay. It was hell for me, but I can't imagine what it was like for him to come to terms with. His partner was whisked away to a hospital an hour away, possessed by an evil illness and his new-born daughter was also away from him. They developed a really close bond in those early days because when he'd visit he'd care for Aarya that whole time, which was sometimes several hours a day. I resented that he was good at it. He'd always be able to stop her crying and get her to burp when winding her. The reason she cried with me wasn't because I was a bad Mum or not doing it properly, it was because she could sense my upset and frustration.

I am forever grateful that my immediate family were there for Dan. A special relationship developed between him and my Father because he'd been there before. My Father was a huge support for him, as were my Mother and Sister. They gave him hope and reassurance that it was temporary and I would get better. Until then, they were there for us.

I said some horrible things to my family and the staff during my time on the M&B unit, some were obvious cries for help. Here's some examples;

'I just want me and Aarya to go to sleep and never wake up.'

'I'm having thoughts of pushing the pram in to the road.'

'She deserves someone who cares, I'll never get better.'

'I'm not going to wash her bottles so she gets ill.'

'I'm thinking of putting a grape in her mouth so she chokes.'

'Take her away!'

Words cannot describe how awful it makes me feel reading some of these things back. It breaks my heart! Sharing this is not intended to shock, it is intended to educate. If I can help one person by identifying something in themselves or someone else, then this is worthwhile. Of-course I feel guilt for Aarya, that I wasn't there for her, for my Mother & Father having to go through it twice, and for Dan having this experience of Fatherhood. But... and there's a big but... I chose to get better, everything happens for a reason. My reason is to help other mums, to change the way the system works and create a better future.

I want to point out the main aspects I remember about the care I received. I felt that it wasn't specialised or personal. There's a motto in our healthcare system about putting the patient at the centre of their care, this didn't happen for me. I was lumbered with several different labels, constantly judged on everything I did or said and was told I was too ill for therapy. The following week I was discharged because I was supposedly well enough to go home. This made me lose faith in the system for a while, although I have since been building this back up. I didn't realise my situation was fairly unique. Some people live and breathe the values of their job and are a true inspiration. I have huge respect for individuals with these kinds of roles as they are incredibly tough. Families of patients have high expectations, quite rightly so and they often have no choice but to trust in the professionals. This is why taking the time to support your loved ones and really listen to what they need is fundamental. Also bringing more options for counselling to these types of facilities could save so much heartache and millions of pounds. Prevention is better than cure.

Homeward bound. That familiar panic was there again because I was informed that I was being discharged. The M&B unit had been my home for several weeks, so it was a big deal. It didn't take me long to get back in to my obsessive, Mrs Particular mode. I was happier though at home, more relaxed. I was functioning on some level of normality rather than a zombie like state. This time coincided with a family death which was tragic, yet it snapped me out of selfish mode. I began realising that it wasn't about me and my problems anymore, I needed to step up and be there for my family. It also coincided with Aarya learning to smile and start giving something back. This saw a huge shift in me because for the first time in a long time I started to enjoy and notice the little things. As you'd imagine the transition from unit to home wasn't all plain sailing. Dan and I had a hard time getting used to living together as three. I really battled with the demons in my head and found it extremely hard to let go of things. We had arguments a lot, and I frequently stormed out of the house to the park, leaving Aarya with Dan. For me this was a way of coping. Sometimes I just had to remove myself from the situation and I'm so grateful I was able to do that.

I began having some private counselling at home which was another game-changer for me. Before having Aarya I started training to become a counsellor because I really valued its place in society. I now value it more than ever having been both the patient and the therapist. I learned so much from my sessions not just about dealing with my emotions, but my counsellor helped me become a better mother to Aarya and partner to Dan. Please don't underestimate the strain something like this puts on a relationship. It's okay to admit things aren't great, the sooner you do that, the sooner you can get help and feel better.

It came to light following my discharge from the unit that I had something called Retained Placenta, this is where part of the Placenta remains in your womb. Having researched this, there are lots of symptoms I experienced which impacted upon both my physical and mental health as a result. Moving on now to talk about my recovery, it was much slower than I expected but it did happen. I eventually saw the light at the end of the tunnel. I was able to wean myself off my medication fully by 18 months post-labour. Aside from a few minor side effects of this, I felt far more human for doing so. I was beginning to get, 'Me,' back again and my friends and family could see that too. I finished my counselling training, started helping others and made a name for myself in the world of Maternal Mental Health. I have been lucky enough to go to The Houses of Parliament twice, have spoken at events and featured in numerous articles/interviews. There is always hope, sometimes you can't see it but after a storm there is always calm. That is when you can appreciate the beauty in everything and learn from what went wrong. Structures can be put in place.

So what really helped me see the light?

- People not judging me
- People being patient and understanding
- An amazingly supportive partner and family
- My counsellor

- Learning something new/having an opportunity to grow (outside of my role as Mummy)
- Sharing my experience with others so we didn't feel alone
- Helping others
- Getting outside whenever I could
- Connecting with nature (the sea mostly!)
- Eating the right nutrition
- My CPN (Community Psychiatric Nurse)
- Aarya (we realise now that she was both the cause and the cure)
- Mindfulness and Meditation
- Good quality sleep

It's still too soon to know if we'll have another child or not, Aarya is now three years old. The irony of what happened is that we now know so much. We understand what help there is out there and know what worked for me. It's a decision I'm not yet ready to make. What I will say is that Aarya is a happy, intelligent and confident little girl. We are super close now, and she reminds me every day. I am grateful that her early life doesn't seem to have affected her, I try so damn hard to make up for it. Dan and I are now able to enjoy being together and being a family. It's all worked out for the best. After having Aarya we were due to get married but understandably this didn't happen when we intended. Now we get to have Aarya as our Bridesmaid and she'll be old enough to remember it. That is a blessing to me.

Sara - Only Human Therapy / email: sara@onlyhumantherapy.com

Ruby's Story

The Crash

It was 7.30am on a normal working day and I was in a tearing hurry to get to work. I had to be there first, I was the boss after all, I must lead by example. I was gathering my things together, bracing myself for the day – smart suit, check. Handbag, check. Briefcase, check. Keys, check. Make-up perfect, check. Right – good to go! I took a deep breath in and started my morning self-talk. It will be okay, you can do this, it's only 8 hours, stay calm, it's just a job, how hard can it be?

Suddenly, the room started to spin and the light faded, my knees felt like jelly, my body had no strength and I couldn't breathe. Wheezing badly, I slowly crumpled onto the floor like a stack of children's bricks and ended up sprawled across the hall carpet. To stop the spinning, I lay as still as a corpse, hanging on to the edge of the doormat. My chest burned painfully – everything else was muted. Eventually, the sound of the post arriving registered dimly, but I was too frozen to call for help. I was paralysed with a nameless sense of dread. This was it, I was dying – with no warning, I was leaving the world.

Silently, I prayed to a God I didn't believe in, please just make the pain stop, let it be over. The world turned black.

Time passed, the sun started to move, shining through the windows onto my back. I woke up groggy. Not dead then? Maybe just a heart attack? Daring to move my arm I saw that an hour had passed. The phone rang and with a super-human effort, I crawled over to reach the handset. I had the keys to the bank and by now the staff were waiting to get in. Mumbling only that I was not coming, I laid back down onto the floor, feeling very ill and very frightened.

Overdraft

All of my life I had been prone to bouts of low mood, anxiety and occasional insomnia, so it was not unusual to feel low. The nine years preceding this day had passed quickly but were filled with consistently high levels of both personal and work-related pressure. If you added up all the main acknowledged stressful events, I had ticked them all, some more than once. Death of a close friend, marriage, change of job (11 consecutive promotions), several house moves (geographical relocations), loss of a baby, examinations, long distance commuting, financial worries, work place bullying and a very lazy husband added to the mix had not helped.

Finally my coping mechanisms had failed me, and my body had decided; enough was, enough. Something clearly had to give and so there it all began, that April day when my ordered little world crashed.

That day was the beginning of a long and challenging journey from what can only be described as a complete nervous breakdown. Enough stress had been piled on me to make a business giant quake, but I just didn't see it. Sure, I felt unhappy and anxious at times, especially recently, but wasn't that just how life was? In my mind, that was completely normal, I thought that hobbies were for the unambitious people of the world with too much time on their hands; holidays were for studying and revising, commuting time was there to give me chance to listen, to work or to catch up on missed sleep; weekends were for household chores.

Crisis management

My first instinct was to call my Dad. I managed to catch him at home and apparently told him, 'I wanted to die.' He was very calm and gentle with me, telling me to take deep breaths, to stay where I was and that he would be on his way immediately. He didn't ask any questions or give me any other advice, just assured me that he was coming. It was as if he was expecting my call. Perhaps he was.

Once Dad had arrived and my husband had come home, I agreed to see the local GP. Strangely, he came to the house and sat with me for ages talking about how I felt and listening to my symptoms, letting me sob and snivel. I didn't know at the time that he had battled his own mental health demons and was therefore more than sympathetic to anyone presenting with such acute symptoms. He convinced me to take some time off work and gave me a sick note, I had recently been on holiday and we agreed we would cite a possible foreign tummy bug as the reason for my absence. I was utterly shocked at my lack of, 'self-control,' and it was so out of character for me to not want to work that I was adamant that this episode remained private. My husband seemed to think this was the best approach; he was terrified seeing me act so illogically (his words). I was given some medication for anxiety and finally managed to eat something and eventually went to bed hoping for a better day the next day.

Shaky foundations

I am the middle child of 3 children, all born within 4 years to my naïve parents. Mum and Dad met and married in a whirlwind romance of only 5 months in the 60s. It was a passionate affair that these days would probably have burnt out quickly with the harsh reality of co-habitation. However, for whatever reason – moral or social restrictions possibly – they got married very quickly. It was a classic case of marry in haste repent at leisure, and on the way bringing 3 children into the world. I honestly cannot recall a time when they were happy for more than a few weeks. My earliest memories of family life revolve around bitter arguments, tense conversations, silences and tears. My mother cried bitterly and often, my father had a foul temper, around which we all tiptoed. Other times, he would be charming and expansive, and bring up fabulous gifts, but we were all a little afraid of his unpredictable moods. My elder brother was a difficult hyperactive child; my younger sister had a naughty, cheeky personality. She could and would charm the birds out of the trees to get her own way. There in the middle, was me. I suffered from cyclical vomiting from a very young age; this was never properly diagnosed but had a big impact on my life and indeed the family as a whole. I always felt I was a nuisance and that somehow it was my fault. I tried hard to make up for this by being a helpful, polite child, and tried to ease any difficulties between my parents if I could. I am quite sure I was no angel, but I was always called, 'the good one,' or the, 'clever one,' which of course I lapped up, thus perpetuating my self-effacing behaviour and the sense that being reliable was my role in life.

My parents both worked hard to give us all the things they hadn't had as children, who grew up during the war years. We moved into a new house in a respectable suburb, we had a good car, holidays, and nice clothes. My maternal grandparents lived close by and we saw them often. My Mother was a senior teacher in our primary school; we had lots of friends locally and a secure routine, despite the tense atmosphere at home.

We bumbled along as a family like this until I was about 6, when my father decided to better himself, returning to college as a mature student so that he could later train as a teacher. This must have been very difficult for him as he was mainly uneducated, for a number of sad reasons which I wasn't aware of then. It was a stressful time; my mother had won a scholarship to grammar school and her parents had scrimped to make sure she was well dressed. She would have found the exams easy and yet she was working full time while bringing us up, mainly alone, whilst he worked shifts and went to night school. Resentment was rife on both sides. However, Dad managed to pass his exams and was accepted onto a degree course.

To this end, the whole family moved from our secure little bungalow in the suburbs to a small village in rural Wales. My father enrolled in University nearby and my mother gave up her job and friends to help us settle in. This was a very unhappy time for me. I missed my predictable routine at junior school, my friends and my grandparents. My parents bought a huge rambling house which needed a lot of work and at the beginning, I had to share a room with both siblings – so I didn't get much peace or indeed much sleep. At school, things were also tricky; we couldn't speak Welsh and were generally much better educated than the local children. Even at 7, I had a reading age of 11 or 12, could speak a few words of French and was generally good at all subjects. My mother was a great teacher after all.

School can be a brutal place – there I was, small, English, clever and, 'posh.' A bully's dream! Luckily I was saved from the worst of it by the Head Teacher, who placed me in the most senior class he could where he kept an eye on me. Eventually, I did make some friends and settled in, but it was very hard, and I felt as if my life had been turned upside down, which it had! When I was 10 years old it was decided that it was time for me to move up to secondary school. I was bored and needed a challenge. At the time I was pleased I was doing well and quite proud that I was seen as clever. Sadly, I was not socially able to cope with being the youngest and smallest in the year of a large comprehensive. I had left all my classmates behind, so I was now really on my own. My older brother naturally, was horrified that I was only a year below him – so resolutely ignored me and left me to cope alone.

Over the next 4 years I was bullied by some of the older girls from our village, mainly during times on the school bus which was an unsupervised 30 minutes both morning and night. It began quite subtly but steadily progressed from verbal insults, swearing, mocking and generally belittling comments to full blown physical aggression both in and out of school. Physically, I was a late developer, and hopelessly shy. As neither parent was working for a while, we were always short of cash – I wore home-made clothes to school and carried a satchel (so un-cool). I even wore white knee socks and a vest until I was 14! I was desperately self-conscious and hated looking different, nobody at home seemed to notice how odd I looked in comparison to other pupils of a similar age. Eventually my younger sister demanded a better uniform and of course I then got one as well and was transformed. At last I fitted in a little. My parents finally broke up during my last year at school and this was a blessed relief as at least arguments were fewer, although it left my mother coping with 3 teenagers and her demanding job.

As with all bullies, as soon as I stood my ground and fought back, they gave up and looked elsewhere, unfortunately, a large worm of self-doubt and diffidence was now well entrenched in my psyche.

Paying back the debt

After the initial terrifying panic attack, the time off work allowed me to gain a little perspective. Me being so driven, I was anxious to return to work – only to find myself crying in the ladies and generally acting like a mad woman. I was a blubbering, neurotic mess.

At home I couldn't relax, at work I couldn't function, I did not eat much and couldn't sleep without pills. In a very short space of time my clothes began to hang loosely around my waist and I looked haggard and my hair began to fall out.

My affable, laid back husband was absolutely no help; he really wasn't used to me, 'not coping.' He often complained I didn't know how to relax, and he was of course, correct. Sadly, I didn't know what that felt like. I had no real hobbies anymore; there had been little time for play. Both our families lived a fair distance from us and we often travelled at weekends to visit. I was an Aunt by now and tried to support my sister by helping her with the children when I could. It wouldn't occur to me not to. My parents were not often available both having found new partners after their acrimonious break up. My relationship with my mother was strained, she had suffered her own mental health problems when I was a teenager and I had seen her struggle to recover and felt responsible.

I couldn't go to her. I felt so alone, so ashamed, so disgusted with myself. I had always thought that once I had gained my last promotion, I would feel successful and that life would become easier. Somehow though, I felt that nobody could possibly respect or admire me, I must have miscalculated, I was so unhappy, I just wanted to die. How could I carry on when I felt so ill? I lurched on from minute to minute and the clock took forever to even move a second while my mind whirled around trying to find an answer.

My initial treatment was extremely random. Our local GP was a kindly gentleman type; he tried CAT therapy and started me on anti-depressants. The self-reflection aspect of the therapy was terrifying as all I could see was that I had ended up in a role where I felt unsupported, with a husband who didn't understand, no friends nearby and nowhere to turn. We had a mortgage, a car loan and were always short of cash.

Moving house repeatedly and paying for our own wedding recently had left us with no savings, living from payday to payday.

There was particularly grim session with the GP, where he hinted rather quaintly as he was renewing my prescription for the pill, that perhaps he shouldn't, as having a baby might be a good idea in order to regulate my hormones and, 'give me a focus.' Apart from wanting to kill him, I now realise he was out of his depth and had not heard a thing I had been saying. I mentioned that my employer gave me full BUPA care as part of my remuneration package – my initial idea was to see someone more skilled and experienced without a long wait.

This news must have been the answer to everyone's prayers as I was very soon whisked into a private hospital some 60 miles away. For some reason that escapes me, I was admitted at the weekend, taken in by my husband who seemed relieved he wouldn't have to miss work. After the basic admission process was completed, i.e. filling in a form and giving them proof of my BUPA cover, he left me to it. My so-called loving husband didn't want to let his football team down by not playing his regular weekend game. I will never forget how utterly rejected and humiliated I felt that day. It was an all-time low point in my life. My own husband felt it was more important to play football than to comfort me. By this stage, I was under no illusion about his ability to help much but I was bitterly hurt by this, I felt worthless. Mortified as I was, I was adamant that my work would not know the real reason I was off ill. Strangely they did not seem very interested, as long as the sick notes were provided; they just carried on paying me.

So there I was in my expensive private room without my shoelaces, any scissors or even a headache tablet. The weekend staff had put me on the, 'suicide watch,' so I was forced to keep my bedroom door open all the time. There was no privacy and pretty much nobody to talk to, all the counselling, psychiatry appointments and group sessions took place during the week so there was nothing at all happening, I was observed but left to my own devices. I didn't really know at that stage what would happen at the hospital, it was all very vague; it felt as if a penal sentence had been passed on me. High-class punishment, admittedly, with my own bathroom and beautifully landscaped gardens, but my idea of hell.

The utter sickening shame of being in a, 'mental home,' was distressing. I lay on my bed, not sleeping and panic stricken. How could I ever recover? Would I ever sleep again? Feel normal again? Work again? Anxiety snowballed, and my mood spiralled ever lower – I envisaged losing our home, being unemployable with, 'breakdown,' plastered all over my medical notes for the world to see. My colleagues would laugh at me; my family would be ashamed. Enough, I wanted to die. Please just let me die, I sobbed and drivelled until somebody came and gave me a pill to make me sleep.

By the Monday morning I was so frustrated and angry I was ready to discharge myself, but of course I was stranded there with no cash or transport, so I had little choice other than to accept the situation, at least temporarily. At last, my allocated mental health nurse arrived and explained how everything worked. He was called Eddie, a calm and gentle Irish man with a lilting accent which was soothing to just listen to. Eddie showed me around properly and gave me an outline of how things worked. In tiny increments, my crushing anxiety started to ease, he was very kind and calm. Other patients returned after being at home for the weekend and were very welcoming. They were all happy to share their own individual woes, which were many and varied. I had been admitted to a mixed acute ward, so there were patients suffering from eating disorders, alcohol problems, exhaustion, PTSD as well as depression and anxiety. It took a few days, but I slowly began to feel that, 'breaking down,' as I saw it, wasn't perhaps shameful. Clearly other people had done it and survived.

My goal was to get released from hospital and be back at work as soon as I could. I hated being at work though, and it made me shudder to even think about the effort of trying to hold it all together again. Fairly quickly though, I started to realise that I really did need professional help. I began to see a really talented psychologist who explained what stress did to the body physiologically.

Slowly it all started to make sense. He encouraged me to talk about the past and helped me see how I had created a prison for myself, based on my childhood survival mechanism of people pleasing. This made me realise that I had been living my life waiting for some kind of magic seal of approval to arrive that would at long last make me feel good about myself. He listened to my story and asked many pertinent questions, as I talked, I started to understand, and it gave me other ideas about how to see things. He gave me biological facts and logical reasons for how I was feeling. He reflected back on my successes in life and made me see that I was far from a failure, rather a victim of coping too well and doing too much. He told me that, 'depression was the curse of the strong,' and this made me feel a little better. This was a logical explanation that I could relate to and slowly the shame started to ease. There was no false sympathy, no promises that it would all magically disappear, just intelligent and gentle discourse.

Challenging though it was, I found myself letting the pain out, of course I cried buckets, oceans even, but that was a massive release. As part of my overall treatment plan, I exercised in the gym, swam, went for walks, was forced to eat regularly, learned to breathe and did some meditation with the group. Oh yes, there were the obligatory craft sessions. I was very sceptical about this, having been able to sew my own clothes since I was 10 years old, but I started a handmade patchwork quilt that first week and it now sits proudly across my bed. Each little hand sewn shape reminds me of the slow but steady progress of healing. It makes me smile and reminds me that progress is often just that, building blocks. Some pieces joined together easily, some tricky bits took longer and needed unpicking to get them right, but in the end, it was completed. It's not perfect but I like that about it, as well.

The other inmates/patients were supportive; we helped each other through the aftermath of tough therapy sessions, sleepless nights and later on, the fear of going it alone in the big bad world again. I certainly didn't want to be admitted to a mental health unit, but in retrospect, I was lucky that I was given that period of time away from everyday pressures, to begin healing. It was apparently okay to just be, to exist, not to be endlessly doing... I think it was the first time, if ever, that this had occurred to me.

After being discharged once and readmitted, I was properly discharged from hospital after about 8 weeks and slowly tried to begin coping alone. I had some fantastic help from an old family friend who I stayed with for a while, it was a safe place, as at first I couldn't be left alone; I was still suicidal and had been given sleeping pills which gave me a blessed 8 hours of sleep and remission from my roller coaster emotional state. She was amazingly gentle and kind and upbeat – despite having two young children to look after – she was so positive I would recover, if I just gave myself time and I began to believe her.

Eventually I went home and was given a lot of outpatient support, my family were also supportive although I found this hard to accept. Slowly I began to regain some equilibrium. Progress was maddeningly slow and there were plenty of dark days where I felt that I hadn't moved on at all, the panic would surge over me again and I would be rendered physically and emotionally paralysed for a while. At times I remained haunted by the idea I had failed utterly and could see little point in life without the reassurance of an important job and the ego boosts that constant progression through the ranks had given me for some time. Over time I had lost the art of enjoying myself – just for the sake of it. My main relaxation had always been to escape into a good book, it helped me to detach from stress and importantly to get to sleep, one of the cruellest aspects of this depression was that it robbed me of my concentration, I could just about get through a magazine article but holding the plot of a novel in my head was now totally beyond me so I had little to distract me at first. I wasn't a big fan of television, so evenings were difficult whilst my energy was so low. I plodded on with my sewing and tried puzzles to keep my mind from spinning around in circles but I found it very hard. I tried twice to go back to work despite medical advice. It was clear I wasn't coping as I still had trouble with mood swings. There were days when the slightest little frustration would send me back to bed, hiding from the world. I did resume work after about 3 months, but it was obvious I wasn't coping as the boss, so I was moved to a much larger branch where I was second in command. I knew nobody there and felt like I had a big sign on my forehead announcing my recent collapse, it was very hard to fit in, and I felt I was being punished and that my hard-earned status was no longer appropriate. None of the more junior staff knew what had happened; they felt awkward talking to me as I was clearly unwell, still pale and skinny. Largely I was ignored, which did little to help me feel settled or to concentrate on my work. I had usually managed to motivate a happy and productive team, so this was torture for me.

After a few weeks, a senior colleague spoke to me. His wife suffered mental health problems and he spotted that I wasn't recovering. He negotiated on my behalf, and with my union, I agreed to take a redundancy package. One morning I went to work as normal, teeth firmly gritted, but determined to get through the day, by lunchtime, I had cleared my desk, returned the keys and was escorted quietly from the premises. That was just the way it happened in banking, just in case you committed fraud in your last moments... my fabulous career was over just like that.

Staying in Credit

Recovery from a severe bout of depression was not a smooth process. There were lots of set-backs. Days when I really couldn't see any point in carrying on as the mood swings and blackness seemed unending. However, the weeks were punctuated by little chinks of hope and light here and there. Gradually the chinks got larger and I found that some days I could see a future.

During the first few months after leaving my job, there were many, many long phone calls to the Samaritans. I was at one stage, so much of a regular that I could recognise all the volunteers by voice. It was a magical lifeline and I will never forget how much that lack of judgement and gentle support helped me face up to the future. Further down my road to recovery I became a volunteer myself and found it so life affirming to offer that same support to others in need. People don't always need advice. Sometimes all they really need is a hand to hold, an ear to listen and a heart to understand them.

I would say that overall it was about 5 months before I was able to cope with the idea of work again. I had applied for a couple of jobs during this time and came very close to being taken on by a progressive and innovative American company. It was a job that seemed made with me in mind and I was very excited about the notion of using some of the skills I had gained in my very varied roles with the bank. I was seconds away from being offered the job but when I asked for a modest salary package they very openly reconsidered as they felt my self-esteem wasn't in, 'the right place.' What a salutary lesson! They were right of course, it took me a long time to realise that I had been very good at my job in the bank and that my skills and experience were worth a lot out there in the real world.

Soon enough, I did get another job and began to rebuild my working life. Luckily the boss was a good sort and the team was small but welcoming. The work wasn't especially challenging, but it felt good just to get back into the workplace and earn my living again.

Since recovering I have had a very varied career and now work in the private medical world, having retrained a few years ago. Working for yourself is no easy option, but I feel I have more control over my life. I eventually learned to ski – a long held dream. This gives me so much joy that I wonder how my life might have been if this had happened earlier. Trial and error have shown me that the most effective antidote to my anxiety seems to keep my mind occupied and to plan things to look forward to. I make time for myself, to have a massage, buy a bunch of flowers, have a coffee with a friend, read a book (such joy) or just take a nap if I need one. On low days I look for little things to focus on and be grateful for to maintain my mood. Of course, there is nothing wrong in having a duvet day and opting out of life now and then, we are not robots after all. I know that stress, anxiety and depression are caused when we are living to please others and I try hard to keep a balance. That diffident child within me can say no and often does.

There is no real end to my story, I still struggle with low mood at times, but I am not as scared, and anxiety no longer owns me. I can reach out for help without shame. It helps me massively to know that nearly two out of three of us experience mental health problems in the course of our life. Every single person on this planet is unique and so is their experience with mental health. On darker days, I try to remember that this too shall pass (Persian fable); it might hurt like passing a kidney stone, but it will pass.

Awareness of mental health and the negative impact of stress has advanced greatly since I was first unwell, and it is much easier to access effective self-help strategies. Simple resources like Facebook groups, mindfulness Apps, a good diet and some exercise can transform the way we feel. There are some excellent self-help books out there, most of which I have read at some stage, and do re-visit if I feel the need. At times, I feel the need to unload and will see a private counsellor which works for me. I lean on carefully chosen friends now and then, as they do me. After all, this is what true caring is all about, letting people see the real you and allowing them to care.

My Statement

Self-love can be learned. Emotional journeys are rarely linear. It took a long time to become unwell and form self-destructive habits, so it took a long time to recover. If you are having a difficult time, please reach out and keep reaching until you find what you need. There are wonderful people out there. I am sending love to everyone who is trying their best to heal from the things they do not discuss.

John's Story

My name is John Clark and I want to share with you my story.

I originated from a very unsettled childhood to being bullied as a young kid at school, to becoming a bully myself and landed myself in a prison. Over the coming years I developed many different kinds of mental health problems which severely impacted my life. After many years of therapy, I can safely say now that I've overcome the worst of it. I now own and run several businesses and would say that I am successful. I thoroughly enjoy helping people achieve their dreams. It's a real honour being part of this book as I really feel that these stories can help you overcome any adversity you're going through. I really do hope to help inspire you to get the right help.

About me

For the last 9 years I have suffered with severe anxiety, OCD and related depression. I have been on life's biggest journey of self-discovery & self-development.

The last few years I've been really trying to understand and figure out why I suffer with these conditions. One of the things I have learnt is that I suffer from something called harm OCD which is a very debilitating condition when you have it, if you don't get help. I don't think it will ever really go away but it's manageable, if you look after yourself. I'm not going to lie, I think it's been pretty tough, I've had to overcome so many different obstacles with my sheer determination and desire to never give up. I'm here today writing and being part of this amazing book with some of the most amazing people.

Let me tell you a little bit about what harm OCD is, it's something that not many people have heard of, it's a form of OCD where intrusive thoughts come into your head at the most ridiculous times that hold the belief that you will either harm yourself or someone else. A sufferer would be someone who would have an image or a thought pop-up in their mind which would lead them to have an anxiety attack or make them feel really uneasy. It also leads to people feeling ashamed, I've heard many people have different types of conditions where they think they're a monster or they think they could be a monster. Quite often I've heard stories of people who are religious and may have said a bad word about their god and then they think their god heard them, and then that makes them feel like they're going to be in trouble as though they've done something wrong. It sounds irrational to some people and they think, "don't be so silly," but to others it's very, very serious.

Someone who doesn't suffer with this condition would have an intrusive thought but would let it go because it's irrational, for someone who is suffering with this condition they would wonder why they had that thought and they would start to obsess. When you're severely suffering, you would be a type of person that would be very analytical. You would constantly be thinking about what if, what if I was that, what if I did do that, but in reality you wouldn't do any of that as people with harm OCD have never acted on any of their thoughts, the actual fact of the matter is that they are actually more caring than an average person.

This condition leads to severe panic disorder, avoiding situations, creating rituals and habits and it can ruin your life if untreated. One of the things that it mostly affects is your social life, you stop going out as you avoid situations all the time. For me it had a massive impact on my family home life, I was trying to be so strong, but I couldn't. Things would get so bad that I would have to sleep downstairs on my own and make up so many different excuses as to why I'm sleeping downstairs, but the truth was I was having a nightmare constantly every day. I would quite often have the same dream, in this dream I was in a fire or I was being attacked or there was something violent happening. As you can imagine, I'd wake up feeling very uneasy. Some nights I would wake up having a severe panic attack where I couldn't breathe and I'd run all the way down the stairs, and I didn't even realise what happened when I realised where I was and that I wasn't in my bedroom, I would then just break out crying. Emotionally this was absolutely killing me as I didn't feel like a man anymore and everybody was down around me.

The only way I can describe it is imagine having a nightmare but being awake the whole time, that's what it's like for someone who's suffering with this kind of OCD. It was really hard as I felt like I had to pretend all the time, really underneath it all I didn't really have much confidence as I had so much low self-esteem. Everybody around me thought I was so confident, but I wasn't, and I would really be struggling inside.

I discovered what OCD was a few years ago, I really didn't have any idea that you could get it with thoughts. I thought OCD was about having to wash your hands many times a day or making sure the doors locked, but there's so many different variations to this disorder. I was in a long-term relationship and was running two different businesses - some would say I was under quite a lot pressure, but I was really struggling. I was absolutely exhausted all the time as I had to keep busy constantly to avoid having any thoughts, keeping busy would mean no time for silly thoughts. I knew that if I stopped I would start having intrusive thoughts and I was so scared. The thoughts that I was having felt so real, I used to think that there was something seriously wrong with me. I thought I was a danger to others and a danger to myself. In reality these were just thoughts, but I didn't understand why I was having them. This condition was making my work life a nightmare as I was really finding it hard to go into customers houses and carry out the surveys and trying to sell. Anxiety was really holding me back in life and my low self-esteem meant that I didn't value myself. I had so many limiting beliefs. If only at the time I thought that if I didn't have this kind of condition, I would be so much further ahead in life.

A positive spin to mental health

If I was to say one thing that was good about having anxiety, it's that it can give you the drive and determination to overcome other aspects of your life. By it giving me the drive to go and become super successful, anxiety is giving me the desire through the fight or flight mode to not give up. It's really important to look at things from different angles. I could write this book and tell you how bad my life is but that would be a lie, I have developed a way and a strategy to enhance the anxiety and channel it in the right avenues. Business, helping others and fitness.

When I was going through different types of therapy one of the things that my therapist made me do was to write a timeline of my life. This helped me to identify and link where I may have got the anxiety from. See, we're all born babies, we're all born equal and the same and it's about our environment we are brought up in. That doesn't mean to say our families, it could mean being bullied at school, it could be an incident or a trauma like being involved in a car crash. Maybe being involved in some physical violence and being a victim – this would all play a key part in the future. From doing the timeline I can now understand why I have some of these issues; whilst I was growing up I went through lots of different traumas. I also made some really bad decisions which had an impact later on in life, I always remember everybody telling me that, one day you will regret it.

Growing up

Life for me as a kid was pretty crazy, my mum and my dad's relationship ended at a very young age, my mum would then later marry a man that I called my dad. He was a real role model of someone of that I aspired to be. By the time I was 15 years old they separated and I just went completely off the rails and I made some really silly decisions. In my earlier years in school, I was very badly bullied to the point where I was too scared to even walk outside, in fact I was petrified. I wasn't a violent person and I couldn't even really have a fight. I would say I was brought up properly.

For a good few months I refused to go to school and this led to a build up for so much social anxiety. I would have home tuition but finally I joined a new school. I was really worried about going to a new school, but I did it, I didn't really have a choice. At the school, I started getting into trouble again, I just couldn't understand why I didn't keep my mouth shut, maybe it was just my appearance, I thought this can't happen to me again surely. During the school years, I ended up in lots of different altercations, I learnt how to use my hands and stick up for myself. Being at school these days is very tough. One thing for sure is I didn't want to be bullied again so I ended up hanging around with a group of associates who would become my friends. We all stuck together and we became a group where by no-one would ever give us any trouble. This didn't do me any favours as outside of school we would get into lots of different trouble, from drinking, smoking, taking drugs, carrying out small crimes. I was approaching 16 years old and I devastated my whole family by being sent to prison for a string of offences.

All of my offences were related to juvenile delinquency – drinking, being antisocial and committing silly offences. I was expelled from school and found myself behind bars.

Prison was a very tough environment and a place that no kid would want to end up, it was a very violent place with people being stabbed and attacked nearly every day. It was an environment that I had to adapt myself to and that would mean by looking after myself. Some of the anxiety of being confined stem from being in a cell for 23 hours a day. When I was in prison I made some really good friends, one gentleman in particular was very close to me and we always looked after each other, his name was Dan. A few years later Dan was released from prison which I was unaware of at the time. It was only when I saw his face on the national news that my good friend Dan had been murdered. He was stabbed to death outside a shop and this was a massive wake-up call to me, this also was a contributing factor as to why I really don't like being around knives. I know now that I also suffered with PTSD which is Post-Traumatic Stress Disorder.

When I was released from prison I managed to get myself a job and I did keep my head down, but I couldn't help but get into more trouble. The last time that I was arrested I was 18 years old, and that was the last time. I decided there and then that I was going to get my head down and become someone.

In my early 20s I finally found out what my calling was, I wanted to be a fully qualified plumbing and heating engineer and go about setting my own company up, so I didn't have to take orders from anyone.

I hated authority. I moved myself out of my hometown to a place where I could get my head down, study, learn, educate and execute my plan on becoming a successful plumber.

My first ever real OCD discovery

When I first discovered I was suffering with this really rare form of OCD, I was living with a girlfriend and I was about 23 years old. I was quite happy as I had just set up my first business and everything was going really well. I started getting intrusive thoughts about harm, especially harming others and this was very disturbing, I felt so ashamed of myself. I used to wake up at night with hot sweats and the only way I can describe it is sheer terror. I would panic, run out the room and just burst out crying, curl up in a ball and just cry and cry and cry. I used to cry quietly so I didn't wake anybody up, I just didn't know what to do, I didn't know where to turn.

I started worrying about my health and I would analyse my body every time my heart skipped, through every single feeling in my body I would think that I was about to die. I started to discover that I was suffering from health anxiety. My anxiety and OCD would rotate from one thing to another, it would always catch you off-guard. These were contributing to negative thoughts and intrusive thoughts, I was creating rituals everyday by avoiding situations.

One of the biggest fears was going to the doctor's, I knew I needed to go but I was so worried about telling him what was going on in my head. The fear of being sectioned was my biggest fear, what if I was sectioned? What if I never come out? My mind would race with fear. Going back 9 years from now I don't even think people were discussing mental health in the way that they are now.

I remember on this particular summer's day carrying out the washing up during the morning. My partner was at work and I remember there was a bowl full of knives that I started cleaning and all of sudden, I just froze, then fell to the floor. I burst out crying with sheer exhaustion as I couldn't handle it anymore. I knew there and then I needed help, I needed it more than ever and I needed to come clean.

I quickly stood up, walked from the kitchen to the front room and just fell over into a clothes line full of clothes in that room. I was completely numb, pale white and having a severe panic attack. I was really stuck, and I just didn't know what to do. I was completely numb, pale white and having a severe from the kitchen to the front room and just fell over into a panic attack. I was really stuck, and I just didn't know what to do. One of my coping mechanisms was going to the gym to burn off the excess energy, so I decided to get my stuff together and quickly shoot to the gym. I went on the exercise bike, just spinning the wheel looking around, thinking all I want is to be normal. I just want to be like everybody else. Why is this happening to me? I managed to reach out to some of my family members and that night I admitted myself to hospital and made a decision that I needed help, I needed to go away. I quickly spoke to psychiatrists and they diagnosed me with severe anxiety disorder then sent me off to go and get some instant therapy. The waiting list for therapy was an absolute joke, at the time I wasn't aware of any other charities and what other help was out there until I discovered self-development. I started to read as many books as I could on self-development and business development to help me grow further. I wanted to push myself and get the right help I wanted and needed. All I wanted in life was to be super successful.

Getting ill again

It was about 2 years ago, I started having a very bad time and I was feeling very poorly again. I was lying in a bath and I remember breaking down and crying and sobbing my eyes out, I just didn't know what to do. It was the worst I had ever experienced it. I quickly searched on YouTube for a bit of support and I came across a video by a guy named Adam Shaw who owns a charity called the Shaw Mind Foundation. His story was almost a spitting image of mine except he didn't go through any trauma at the level I did, he suffered with a rare form of OCD where he used to have intrusive thoughts about strangling other people for no reason or contemplating suicide. He publicly came out on TV and so much awareness for people was raised. Because of this video I managed to get the help I needed, I reached out and found a specialist OCD company who did a week retreat, whereby you would go to visit them down south, spend the week with them educating you on why you have these issues. I'm not going to lie, this for me was make-or-break in my head, I just didn't know where to turn and all I wanted was to just be normal like everybody else (what is normal?).

Until this point I tried many forms of therapy ranging from CBT, relaxation, technique hypnotherapy, EMDR, none of which worked for me. Don't get me wrong, I'm sure they helped me in some way as I was quickly finding out that I needed to educate myself, I believe personally there are a lot of these conditions and it's just down to understanding your body.

At this point, me and my partner at the time had a new-born baby. I was already under a lot of pressure, work was becoming increasingly more stressful and very hard to manage. I was really struggling with time and I was trying to be as supportive as I could be. I felt like I was really failing, with the birth of my son, the sleepless nights crept in and the support wasn't there from anyone, because all the focus was on the new-born baby which is to be expected. I was just so worried about letting everybody know that I was really struggling. I wasn't sleeping much at all and quite often I would sneak and go downstairs and lay on the sofa where I would just cry and cry and cry. My partner was really struggling and I just didn't know what to do, I decided that I needed help, so I booked into the retreat in Somerset that I'd found. When I spoke to them they fully understood my situation and said they could really help me.

Whilst there, there was a therapy treatment called exposure therapy, this was whereby you would be exposed to physical objects or situations that you may be scared of. One of my biggest fears were knives, well one of them, this was because as a young boy I was involved in a few knife incidents whereby I was nearly stabbed, and I was robbed at knifepoint. I would hide all the knives at home, I would put them in the lower part of the drawer as I was really scared of them. I didn't even know that I was doing this. I would only ever handle knives when no one else was around, again, I didn't even realise that I was doing this.

Having exposure therapy was the right treatment for me. During the week I would have to handle, hold and play about with knives in a controlled environment, it was all about reprogramming the amygdala in my brain. The amygdala is a part of the brain that stores trauma and bad memories so by doing exposure therapy you're rewiring the brain. The thought that I could overcome this part was really exciting for me and I was committed, I was all in, so I tried out this for the week continuously, handling knives, and by the time I left the therapy my views and fears were massively reduced.

Triggers

Some of the trigger points for me were when I used to watch horror films, that would really trigger my anxiety and OCD and panic and fear. Often, I would find myself removing myself from a room or even making excuses at the cinema to go to the toilet frequently, the fact of the matter is, I was really scared.

Taking it back even earlier, one of the signs was that I used to struggle with travelling, I used to work up in the city as a plumber in my early 20s. This was one of my biggest passions at the time, I just wanted to be a really successful plumber and then later on set-up my own business. I soon gave that up because the anxiety was far too much, I'd be so paranoid and worried about what people thought of me whilst I was commuting that I would have breakouts of sweat and panic and would have to remove myself from the train at nearly every station just to let new people on the train. It would give me a couple more minutes to try and settle into the new environment, but this didn't work. As you can imagine it was becoming a living nightmare, I didn't know what was going on in my mind and I just blamed it all on the past. I felt like it was all my fault and it was some way of punishing me for the way I acted as a juvenile.

I identified that it wasn't the fact of travelling, it was the fact of being confined, now this would potentially go back to when I was in prison, I guess the thing that I know more now than ever it's the fact of sitting there not doing anything. I always have to keep busy and sometimes the anxiety is so severe that reading a book isn't a big enough distraction. Being confined in tight spaces in public transport or stuck on the motorway can be a real pain.

When I turned 30 years old, myself and my partner at the time brought a property in Corfu. I absolutely love this this country but here was another story, I absolutely hated flying, I hated being confined on an aeroplane for so long. I love the country so much that I was committed to flying out there for holidays, I knew that I had to overcome the fear of flying. I wanted to be able to be in a position where I could take my family on holiday, things got so bad for me on the aeroplane that I would be brought to tears for the first 15 to 20 minutes of the flight. My mind would be racing and I was having all these intrusive thoughts like something bad was about to happen. The anxiety was through the roof but after about 30 minutes when the flight was in the air and I was able to walk around, my anxiety would subside. It would get a lot easier and I started becoming myself, I can't explain how good it felt when I was on that plane that I didn't have anxiety even for just a few minutes. I felt like a real man, I felt like a family man. It would feel like a rollercoaster to get back home and I would drink as much as possible, consuming this at the airport, this could be a whole bottle of wine or a pack of beers along with some sleeping tablets. These are the tactics that I used but in reality, I know I shouldn't have done.

I had a lot of shame around me as it wasn't one of those things you can just tell your mates or family (well I was wrong you should). I couldn't say, "hey, I get all these intrusive thoughts and I don't know what to do with them." I was so worried about being judged.

Over the years I had embarked on lots of different therapy, one of the things that would stand out the most is the fact that you shouldn't just give up at the first hurdle. You should see your treatment through and give it a proper go. Look at it in a positive light, yes, this treatment didn't work for you, but you're now one step closer to finding the right therapy.

I've also tried so many different variations to my diet. I have increased certain foods, decrease certain foods, restricted coffee, increased coffee – all of which have benefited me. Some of the best things I've ever done has been limiting the consumption of alcohol and avoiding situations where it will be alcohol fuelled. I choose now to have a glass of red wine and listen to some calming music like jazz.

Self-Help Tips

If you can understand your body and recognise the signals when you're starting to feel unwell, then I think and feel that you can prevent yourself from getting depressed. One thing I did pick up from all the therapy that I had for a few years, was to carry a survival bag with me. Now I must admit I don't really keep this with me as I'm at the other end of the spectrum now, but something that I found really useful was carrying this bag. In this bag it had all the luxuries that would make me feel good, I would have a small bottle of red wine, a set of headphones, some jazz on my playlist and some sweets – these are all luxuries and comforts for me. I knew that if I was starting to feel a little bit down, I would have a little bit of sugar and have a drop of red wine with a bit of jazz in my ear and that would make me feel really calm and relaxed.

I think it's really important to find out what works for you and what doesn't work for you and this can be done by keeping a diary. A daily journal of how you feel throughout the day, this could be done in hour segments. If you carried this out for 28 days, imagine how useful that information would be? If you knew that drinking a coffee around lunchtime made you feel very anxious or drinking a coffee before a meeting, you would then learn to take it out. It does take you time to understand and learn about your body, but my experiences taught me to keep trying new things all the time, and track things and you will eventually build up your own system whereby you know your limitations.

Another thing that I have learnt is to network, especially if you're in business, even if you're not, make sure you're very social, look after yourself, make sure you're eating food, make sure you're working out, make sure that you're in a very good relationship. If you're not, then look to change things up. If your job is creating too much stress you can ask yourself some serious questions such as, "is this worth my health?" I've made many mistakes over the years and feel that I can't possibly make any more.

One thing, if there is anything you take away from reading my section of this book, is that you are not your thoughts, if you were mad, you wouldn't actually know that you were. The fact that you're worrying about anxiety and OCD is because you're a very caring person, no one's ever acted on thoughts. A book that I would highly recommend reading is by Professor Stephen Peters – he wrote the most amazing book called the Chimp Paradox. This book will really help you understand how the brain works, everybody has an inner chimp you just have to feed the chimp in your brain sometimes and then cage it.

Where I'm at now

I am currently in one of the most positive states of mind that I have ever been in, I have learnt over the last few years that to overcome anxiety I need to become confident, to up my game. I'm now in a fortunate position where I can help other people in business create their dreams. I recently launched one of the UK's most inspirational podcasts for tradesmen.

My approach to business development and personal development is relentless, I've never been so committed to growing myself. Writing this book contributes factors that make me move forward, by talking about my experiences, I found that helps me 100%.

In 2018 I decided that I would write a memoir and I launched the book called If I Can You Can, and this book was written to help inspire other people to overcome their adversities. I wanted to share my story to the world. I feel that everybody has a story within and it's really important, as so much healing comes from writing, it's probably one of the best strategies that I could recommend. I really hope that these stories inspire you to get the right help that you may need.

I would like to say one nice thing, never, ever, ever give up on your journey, one thing for sure is that we don't get back our time, that's why it's important to move forward and to try not to dwell on the past and enjoy your life.

John Clarke

Director. John Howard

Author 2018: *If I Can You Can*

Podcast Host: (The Streetwise Tradesmen)

Business Mentor

Suzanne's Story

When I was 18 years old, I nearly lost my life to a sudden massive bilateral Pulmonary Embolism (blood clots in the lungs). I was that, "goody two shoes girl," - I rarely partied, ate healthy, and made being active a priority. So why the hell was this happening to me? I remember the unfolding of June 1, 2011 clearly, struggling to get tiny breaths of air into my lungs with excruciating pain, as the ultrasound tech did her exam on my grossly swollen and purple left arm. She was only a few minutes into conducting the exam before she quickly excused herself to go get the doctor with a look of grave concern in her eyes.

My heart stopped. I remember thinking, "Great. You were too fucking stubborn to get this checked out 2 weeks ago and now you're probably going to die." Dramatic 18-year-old girls, am I right? Anxiety flooded my system, and yet there was some level of consciousness that knew this was not going to be the end of my story.

I had no idea what was in store for me in the years to come. This is my journey of living with a very rare neurological degenerative genetic disease that I was unaware of until the age of 23. I went through many transformative experiences that shaped me into the fearless and confident woman that I am today.

The first culprit blood clot was so long that it extended down almost to my left wrist, up my arm, and across my chest where pieces of clot were dripping through my heart. The doctors said that I was extremely lucky I didn't have a stroke because of how large the clot was as it was pushing back up into my internal jugular vein. Surprisingly my heart did fantastic with all the madness; only one of the valves at the top of my heart was damaged. My lungs were riddled with pieces of clot, but the deposits were spread out enough that neither of my lungs collapsed. It took months of physiotherapy, and religiously taking large doses of Serrapeptase to clear the scar tissue in my arm to gain back most of the normal blood flow to my arm. I had already enrolled to begin my Massage Therapy Diploma that upcoming September – 3 months later, and I couldn't miss out. I spent a majority of the summer of 2011 in hospital undergoing massive amounts of testing to pinpoint a cause for these catastrophic events. Every test came back negative. Multiple CT scans, VQ scans, ultrasounds, colonoscopies, mammograms, ultrasounds, and daily blood work revealed nothing abnormal. Except now my lungs were peppered with patches of dead lung tissue. These inconclusive results were both a relief and a colossal disappointment; they confirmed that I wasn't suffering from any super rare cancers but left me with no known course of action I or my doctors were supposed to take. I had some very dark moments in that hospital. Often at night, my mind would race and would play out possible scenarios of what my future may hold.

At this time, my parents denied that they were aware of any genetic diseases in the family. Years later, I would finally understand why they had chosen to remain silent.

I kept a journal during my stay, which I found to be an essential release whenever things became overwhelming. After a few days, my parents returned to work in our hometown 2 hours away, so I spent a lot of my time without my support system. I was very blessed that a few Edmonton-based family members visited from time to time. At that time in my life, I didn't know that I could ask for help when I was hurting. I had always felt from a young age that it was my duty to never cease helping others. And now, I had found myself in a hospital full of very sick and dying people; all who needed help in one form or another. When I wasn't doped up on morphine, I would visit others. Hearing their story and giving them what encouragement, they were willing to hear, lifted my own spirits. I heard my name called over the P.A. system dozens of times during my stay, calling me back to my room, usually for more testing after I had wandered off yet again.

At the end of the summer in 2011, my new hematologist and pulmonologist decided to give up the search for a cause of the blood clots. I was released from the hospital with instructions to take a daily dose of blood thinners, and to be wary of symptoms appearing again. My 5'5" frame weighed a little over 100 pounds then. Against my specialist's advisement, I moved to prepare to begin my first year of Massage Therapy School. I was desperate to replace the fear of the unknown with some sort of intended focus. I hadn't grasped the concept of needing balance in a person's life yet. I assumed that because I had been able to survive so much of what should have taken my life, I didn't deserve to be, "sick."

At the age of 19, I was so hopeful to have this new beginning of life on my own. Until I ended up in the emergency room with clotting symptoms just 2 months before my first-year exams. This time, it was my right lung bombarded by the clots. Now, I had a specialist team wanting to schedule me for surgery to place a filter at the top of my heart to prevent further damage. I had just embarked on more of a holistic path at this point, so I did refuse the surgery. I didn't fancy the idea of having a foreign object in my heart that may or may not perforate it if they didn't place it correctly. I placed my faith in these doctors to discover why I had been able to clot again despite being on blood thinners. It was discovered that I had been placed on too low a dose of my medication by my previous hematologist. This medication was stopped and instead I had to teach myself how to perform injections twice daily.

I remained hopeful that doctors within the hospital would pinpoint this seemingly elusive diagnosis as I had read that there was a 33% chance of not surviving recurring pulmonary embolisms. I was so fortunate that again, the clots had broken off small enough from my left arm that they didn't get stuck in my heart on their way into my lungs.

I was simply trying to be a responsible young adult, go to college, get a career that I would love, and do my part to better society. This bombardment of blood clots was really beginning to put a damper on that. Regardless of this setback, I requested to be released in time to write my finals. In March 2012, I graduated my first year of Massage Therapy School. I secured my first job ever as a career woman less than 2 months later. I did well for the next 20 months; I was careful with my exercise routine, my diet, and bitterly took my blood thinning medications daily. I did my best to balance out the harsh effects of long-term blood thinner use by seeking out different naturopathic healers, for supplements to support my circulatory system. I built a marvelous, regular massage clientele over the next 2 years. I became accustomed to regularly scheduled specialist visits as every few months I had a test of some sort scheduled to observe the damage left behind in my arm, lungs and heart.

In the summer of 2014, I disregarded my entire medical team. Because of how healthy and fit I was feeling, I decided that I no longer needed to take my blood thinning medications. I had experienced such massive positive results with Access Consciousness and Biofeedback, that I truly believed the treatments had healed whatever had caused those very first blood clots to form 3 years prior. I had hit a wall with the medical community. For years, I had blamed my doctors for not being able to find a diagnosis, so I felt the need to cut them out of my life entirely.

Thankfully, my lung specialist chose not to abandon me, despite knowing the foolish decision I had chosen to make. In a couple months I was admitted to a different Hospital in Calgary under his care. More rounds of tests came with this 10-day hospital stay. It was discovered that I had been throwing small blood clots from my left arm yet again, into both lungs during my medication hiatus. A right heart catheterization revealed that I had also developed CTEPH (Chronic Thromboembolic Pulmonary Hypertension). Because so many blood clots had passed through my heart and deposited into my lungs, areas of my lungs had infarcted leaving behind scar tissue.

At this point, I was frustrated beyond belief. That summer I had felt so surely convinced that I was on the right path to heal my body and had begun taking back some of the time lost during the last 3 years. Instead, I ended up toying with my life by taking it into my own hands. I felt awfully guilty for taking such a tremendous risk without stopping to consider the consequences. I decided it was time to begin digging into our family history on my own. I could no longer ignore my need to understand what was causing such upset within my body. I didn't want to be medication dependent without understanding why. I had now survived three pulmonary embolism episodes, all stemming from my left arm, with no explanation. I pleaded my case to my general practitioner again and asked for a referral to see a geneticist.

As I waited for the opportunity to take my search further, my boyfriend at the time, who had been with me for the past 3 years, decided that it was time to leave. He had tried to leave a few times previously, but always took his words back. This time, it was for good. Like any girl who suffers her first real heartbreak, I was shattered.

At 23 years old I felt completely baffled at what my next step should be. Any time before when I had a new blood clot, my instincts always told me exactly what I had to do. I knew I just had to survive. But this emotional devastation felt so overwhelming compared to all the physical trauma I had experienced. Isn't it a bit eerie that our mind can be powerful enough to demand that our body survive an event that should have indefinitely caused death, but when we suffer an emotional desolation, our heart suddenly has this ability to overrule the mind if we allow it to? It shocked me that I felt more debilitated now than I had any time I spent lying in a hospital bed, wondering if this clot would be the one to end my life or not.

Full-blown panic attacks were a daily occurrence for the first week. My brain and body felt as if it was on fire. My nerves were shot. I was so physically weak, I had to cancel my clients for the first week after he left. I felt such overwhelming shame that a break-up was seeming to cause more pain than anything else that I had already survived. I choked down protein shakes during the day for some amount of sustenance. My usual saviour of listening to binaural beats to soothe my nerves enough to sleep wasn't cutting it this time. So, I turned to alcohol in a frantic attempt to just shut down feeling anything for a while. My nerves were shot. It felt as though my mind and heart had suffered a temporary disconnection. Being on blood thinners, this was a very dangerous road for me to begin down. I am so fortunate that I didn't end up with any internal bleeding during this short phase of my life. I am so grateful that I had an amazing Reiki practitioner who was willing to work on me twice a week for an hour each session. Two weeks later, and I still hadn't heard a word from my now ex. I knew that I needed to pack up the remainder of my things from our old apartment, but I couldn't fathom facing him just yet.

I had only just scratched the surface of allowing myself to fully integrate healing. I hadn't allowed the pain fully in. I hadn't accepted the pain of all that I had gone through at such a young age. I had an, "invisible illness." I didn't feel deserving of being chronically ill. I created the identity that I was stronger and better than any adversity, without stopping to heal emotionally. Now that my heart was broken, I could feel all that undealt-with pain rise to the surface with ferocity. I had chosen to push away all that agony because it was the only way I knew how to survive. But now, there was no escaping any of it. It became very clear to me that I would have no choice, but to actually stitch myself back together. Probably for the first time in my life I asked myself, "what do I need? What do I need to do right now?"

My answer came to me almost immediately, "create space and heal." I felt a rush of soothing peace instantly wash over me. I knew that for the first time in 4 years, I was about to give my soul time to heal.

So, I told my clients that I was taking a temporary stress leave for approximately 2 weeks and I drove back to my hometown of Edson, AB. I remember being shocked at how much relief I felt being physically far away from someone who had caused my heart to shatter. My lungs drew in full breaths of air for the first time in weeks and I could feel those heavy cords begin to break away from my heart.

My best friend Andrew was diagnosed with a very rare disease, Takayasu Arteritis (TAK), around the same time that I had first gotten ill. I guess you could say that idiopathic medical mysteries tend to attract each other. Often, we'd spend a couple hours on the phone together, unaware of our realities. I made the trek to Edson knowing that I would be spending a lot of my time with him. It was here that my path crossed with who I would soon recognize as my warrior.

At one fateful night movie night at Andrew's, a fellow high school graduate who also happened to be visiting Edson at the same time joined us. After everyone else had fallen asleep, I remember him asking if I was doing okay because the sadness I was projecting, wasn't how he remembered me to be. After grabbing coffees at 2 a.m. we found ourselves out of town, parked on the edge of a farmer's field, gazing at the angelic beauty of the stars. I remember witnessing three shooting stars that night. As we shared our current life stories with each other, I discovered that he too had suffered a similar heartbreak 2 years prior. I couldn't shake this undeniable feeling that he felt like home.

I received a lot of flack from some friends and family members, who feared I was going to end up using John as a rebound. But now, as I reflect on this time over 3 years later, I can clearly see that he was placed on my path to help me stitch my heart back together. He went through the typical stage of partying to fill the void he felt after his girl had left. But when he realized that he wasn't healing, he turned to meditation, drawing, and honoring his health. It was only when he began to turn his focus inward that he was able to begin healing his core wounds.

That is exactly what John did for me. As our relationship began to grow so organically, I felt the most alive I had ever felt in YEARS. With John's unwavering support and encouragement, I decided that I would follow through with returning to post-secondary school again

In 2015, I was accepted into a 15-month Cardiology Technologist program. However, two weeks before I was to fly to BC for my clinical rotation, my father hit one of his most manic depressed states yet. He had been diagnosed with Bi Polarism 10 years prior but decided not to continue with medications that were prescribed after his first major manic episode. It was one of the hardest decisions I had to make to leave him behind in another psych ward. It tore my heart open to leave after only being able to have short visits with him in the hospital. I had to trust that he would be taken care of until I could return. I took comfort in the fact that I was able to stay in contact with him almost daily with phone calls to his ward. This was the only way I could show him that he always had my full support. This compounded stress manifested itself in my body in a frightful way - I was unable to fend off a serious staph infection in my left leg from a small cut in my foot. The doctors told me that I was in danger of losing my leg if I didn't allow it time to heal properly. The infection and stress of not being able to be by my father's side impacted my performance greatly during my practicum, but I persevered. My preceptors allowed me to have a stool in my testing room as I conducted stress tests under evaluation, so I could be off my infected foot as much as possible. Luckily, I was able to fly back home three weeks early to be reunited with my father.

Only one month after returning to Alberta, I received notice that there had been a cancellation with the geneticist I had been anxiously waiting to see. My appointment was in two weeks-time. This spurred on my motivation once more, to reach out to distant family members to inquire if anyone else had been exhibiting seemingly idiopathic, and disconnected symptoms.

If I hadn't decided to pick up the phone that day to call a distant cousin of mine in Ontario, I am uncertain if I would be where I am today. On that day I discovered that there is a known and rare disease, caused by a genetic mutation, that runs on my mother's side called Oculo-Dento-Digital Dysplasia (ODDD). I was perplexed as to why I was hearing everything from a cousin that lived on the other side of the country, when for the last 4 years my parents had watched me struggle to thrive. I also learned the very specific reason why my parents had chosen to adopt my younger brother instead of trying for another child after I had been born. All of this was so bittersweet. For the very first time in 5 years, I finally had concrete information that I could work with.

This mutation results in brain signal abnormalities due to malformation of the gap junctions of certain cells either in the womb or can develop late into adulthood. These gap junctions are often permanently closed, preventing any transport of molecules. Thus, affected areas of the body are vast, and it does not present the same for every individual diagnosed. It is labelled as a neurological degenerative disease with currently no known way to predict its progression or treatment for the condition. Essentially, it means that parts of the brain could die faster than normal which leads to systems shutting down earlier than they should as a person ages. In the same breath, a person could be born with a late advancement of the disease as it also affects the development of a child in the womb. Skeletal abnormalities are of the most common noticeable symptoms. It occurs when there is interrupted intercellular communication during the bone remodelling stage in utero. The most common physical traits to be noticed are usually structure related, or with peripheral nerve deterioration such as, vision or hearing loss. At times, the communication in the body can be so disrupted that organs such as the heart, or brain do not fully develop. Less than 300 people have been diagnosed worldwide, with a 1 in 10 million chance of incidence according to the U.S. National Library of Medicine.

I questioned my parents as to why they failed to mention this familial disease when specialists had asked if there were any known diseases in the family back when I was 18. As it turns out, before my parents became pregnant with me, they were advised by genetic counsel that my mother was likely a dominant carrier of the disease, and there was no way to guarantee the severity their child may experience if they received the genetic mutation. Frustration and feelings of betrayal took me a long while to sort through. I also learned that some of my family members carrying the disease were born paralyzed, some lost the use of their legs in their mid 60s, and some had completely unrelated symptoms to paralysis.

When I was born my parents were convinced that I was healthy and didn't carry the disease because I didn't present with the same obvious physical traits of the disease that my mother manifests. This explained why its existence in our family was never spoken of until I confronted them myself 23 years later. Unfortunately, my parents chose to remain uneducated about this condition, so they missed symptoms in my childhood years that could have possibly prevented a lot of unnecessary mayhem in my young adult life.

As I continued to gather information, more puzzle pieces began to align. I had a consultation with the geneticist in November 2016, where we discussed the likelihood that I was carrying this rare mutation. A few months later, I found out that the geneticist had taken my case to the Board of Alberta Health Services where they had agreed to order the appropriate genetic testing. All that was needed from me now was a simple blood test. A couple weeks later, another phone call came, one that changed the course of the rest of my life.

I had tested positive for one of the genetic mutations causing Occulo-Dento-Digital Dysplasia. Specifically, I had a mutation in my GAJ1 gene. She explained to me that it is commonly responsible to also cause progressive leukodystrophy. Leukodystrophies typically lead to the destruction of the white matter throughout the nervous system, often affecting the brain, spinal cord and peripheral nerves. Years of unexplained turmoil were suddenly validated with a mere sentence. We cried tears of fear that day unknowing of what the future may hold.

Knowing now that this mutation was present, my fragile and small bone structure made sense. It finally explained why I had broken and dislocated many bones while growing up. It was also discovered that my collar bone and ribcage had developed too wide within my small frame. So, when I became more active in my young adult years and began to develop more muscle tone, it restricted blood flow to my arms. I am left hand dominant, so this discovery also provided an explanation for why blood clots were always discovered in my left arm only. There wasn't enough space for blood to flow through my major veins with ease, so with repetition I developed clots. It's a short route from your arm veins to the heart, so therefore I put my heart in extreme danger every time I clotted. How interesting is it that my body stared death in it's cold, relentless face many times, all because of a simple mutation within my DNA?

From this point on, I knew that my journey was far from over, but I held on to hope, that I could now do my best to prevent more unnecessary suffering.

I began to inquire what other family members had experienced with this disease in their later years of life. That curiosity was swiftly met with a sense of dread. My mother's father began exhibiting symptoms in his late 50s. Unfortunately, medical experience with this disease in the 1970s was of course far more minimal than today. Unknowingly to them, my grandfather was presenting with Neurogenic Bladder Syndrome which is a condition caused by the nerves along the pathway between the bladder and the brain not working properly. The deterioration continued as he developed symptoms of Spastic Paraplegia, and eventually resulted in the loss of use in his legs. It took him approximately 7 years to become wheelchair bound, permanently catheterized, and living with a colostomy bag. After digesting all this new information, I made a vow to myself that I would do everything in my power to prevent my own body from facing the same fate. On that same day I made a promise to myself and John that I would learn how to heal blood line trauma.

The geneticist had set me up with referrals for a neurologist, a urologist, and an ophthalmologist to observe over the years, to catch any nerve deterioration before it became irreparable, like it had for my grandfather.

An MRI of my brain confirmed that brain signal abnormalities whose patterns matched leukodystrophy were already present in myself. This raised questions if I was experiencing any other symptoms that I had not yet mentioned. I was now forced to admit to a problem that I had been trying to conceal for the past 4 years. Its existence seemed to have no correlation to my blood clotting issues, so when I did voice my concern, it had been promptly dismissed by doctors. The truth was, I had been doing my best to tolerate progressive worsening of incontinence on top of the seemingly idiopathic blood clots. By the age of 24, I had to ensure that a change of clothes was always with me when I left the house. I could feel my self-esteem and confidence wither away with each accident. I practiced Kegels religiously, with hope that it would be enough to provide some sort of relief. Had I known about the existence of this disease 4 years ago, perhaps the scarring of my bladder could have been prevented.

Even with knowing that my body was showing signs already of peripheral nerve deterioration, my referral to the urologist to have this addressed still took 19 months for me to be seen. By October 2018, my bladder control had become very minimal. Even as this aspect of my condition has worsened, John has always been right beside me cheering me on with the most loving support. This has been one part of the condition that has taken the most toll on my mental health. I've struggled deeply with not allowing fear to overtake my thoughts even with my body presenting with signs that could lead to Spastic Paraplegia. Upon seeing the urologist, it was discovered that this consistent level of dehydration my body had succumbed to for years had put tremendous stress on my kidneys. It was made clear that we had to find a solution for these Neurogenic Bladder symptoms in fear of otherwise eventually losing the kidneys. I began self-catheterizing and pelvic floor physiotherapy in December 2018 to cope. It is uncertain of how this nerve degeneration may continue within my body, and my treatment will depend on it.

I have made preventative measures to preserve overall nerve function my new priority. I have began targeting healing my DNA with sound therapy such as singing bowls, tuning forks, and listening to the frequency of 528Hz as I sleep. I have since discovered the healing power of Yoga. Thus, my path crossed with a beautiful soul, named Jeanine. She is a yoga teacher with a burning desire to heal the people within this world, one by one. My story inspired her to share Kangen Water with me; an alkaline rich water that is the very best drinking water because of its incomparable powers of hydration, detoxification, and anti-oxidation. I am so grateful that she has been placed on my path to bring such an impactful healing tool into my life. I believe that its ability to balance out oxidative stress within my body will aid immensely in at the very least, slowing down further nerve loss.

I have learned that I am not in control of my future. All I can control is my reaction to what I am experiencing in each moment.

I realize now that trauma is what strings us all together like pearls on a necklace. We all need a safe place to share our story, so, here I am sharing without shame, guilt or fear. I am grateful that the events in my life led me to discovering the existence of this incredibly uncommon disease relatively early. I know that this genetic mutation will not continue in my family line, it will end with me. I am taking control of my own destiny. There is much of my story left unwritten, and I know that what I have experienced does not define who I am. I am Powerful. I am Fearless.

My perspective on life has shifted massively. I now strive to live within the moment. I may follow in my previous family members footsteps and end up losing my lower body nerve function, or that may never become my story. My life has shaped me to become the woman that I am today. I have many more years left to live on this Earth and I am okay with the uncertainty of what else this disease may or may not bring. I can either choose to embrace the unknown and embark on a mission to become empowered no matter the circumstances, or I can allow fear to paralyze me. I choose Life. What has become most important to me now is to live my best life, and to do it unapologetically. Time is precious. We can never get back spent time. It is my intention to show myself and the world the unimaginable healing capability we all possess.

There is beauty within pain. For without pain, we would never be able to truly appreciate the beautiful and still moments in life.

Suzanne - Facebook: https://www.facebook.com/suzanneglambregts/

Alan's Story

Just a few years ago, I was kneeling in the living room of my family home all alone crying at the situation I found myself in, I felt like I had failed as a husband, father, business owner and as a man in general. I couldn't afford to live in my house and I couldn't afford to sell it either, my business was falling apart and if I got a full-time job instead, the child payments my children's mum wanted would mean I still couldn't afford to make ends meet.

I was pondering and questioning how I ended up in this situation, and why all this shit was happening to me.

I returned home from a year traveling alone, in March 2004, it was the most mind and heart opening experience I had had at that time. I was relaxed, I was happy although I knew I had to find a job, a car and get back to life at home again. After a year of not being answerable to anyone, just friends I made along the way, not staying anywhere longer than 3 months, I felt like I was ready to settle down. Especially after being back living with my parents for a couple of weeks. Back to being asked where I was going, who I would be going with and when I was going to be home. Inside

I was screaming out "I am 27 for crying out loud – not 7 – do you really need to know all this?" I decided I was going to get my own place within a year, I couldn't do it straight away as I had some travel debts to pay and had depleted my savings more than expected and didn't want to rent. I got a job working nights as a truck mechanic as I had been before, and only a few months down the line I had been promoted and paid off all my debts and started to save money.

I worked 4, sometimes 5 nights a week and the weekend I was out with my mates, I was also looking for a girlfriend or a girl I would like to date when I was out, yet I still didn't seem to meet any. Even after travelling I didn't find it easy to meet and get to know girls, I never knew what to say or if I had something to say I would get tongue tied and any words that did come out my mouth sounded a little like the Tasmanian Devil cartoon character. I didn't know why or how to change, let alone if I could, it had always been a challenge for me and it really felt like I just wasn't good enough or I just wasn't attractive to girls. There was a solution known as "internet dating." I liked the idea of being able to chat first, so a girl could get to know me or who I was on the inside and see that I wasn't the kind of bad boy that my girlfriends used to always get hurt by and complain about. I was always the one who picked up the pieces, yet they wouldn't date, even though they would all say that I was a really good guy – to say it confused me was an understatement.

After a lot of online chatting and one or two dates I had gotten quite close to an Asian girl who was studying hotel management in Belgium. She wasn't going back to her family in the summer holidays, so she came to England where we could meet. We got on really well and seemed like we had some things in common, still having a lot to talk about. I went over to Belgium to see her in the Autumn and she came to me for Christmas. We visited each other for a few more weekends and holidays and started to look at what the possibilities were for further developing our relationship.

I bought my house in January 2005, I'd had to move to a different town to make it possible though it was the same travelling distance and time from work as my parents' house.

She was very keen to get married, I did have a few reservations as we still didn't know each other that well. I felt like I was ready to settle down though and in part I was fearful that if I didn't marry her then I may never meet another girl who was willing to settle down with me. We looked at all the different options for visas with her not being a UK resident. We were both wanting a family with two children, and to be self-employed as well as to travel, despite a few cultural differences, language differences and personality differences. Having never had much success with girls and not the greatest level self-confidence I felt like this could be my best chance of a successful relationship. On the next trip I took to Belgium we went to speak to the British Embassy and organised for her to get her visa to come to the UK as a fiancée, part of the rules of this visa was that we had to be married within 3 months of it being issued. I felt it was rushing us a little and I spoke to my parents who said that "you won't really get to know her any better just going there, or her coming here for a few weekends a year," and, "don't worry, if it doesn't work out divorce is much cheaper than it used to be." I still had their support with it.

Not long before she was due to move over, one of my best friends came around to ask if I had considered that I maybe I was making a mistake and that she may be just doing it to get a British passport. I told him that I didn't feel that was the case, even though it had crossed my mind, I was well aware of the risks and thanked him for his concerns.

She moved to be with me in August 2005, and we were married in October 2005, I did have a feeling that it may not be totally right a couple of weeks before the wedding, my family said that it was just cold-feet, and everyone gets that before the big day anyway. One of my stipulations was that her parents had to be there for the wedding, firstly to see their daughter get married and also so that they could meet me, as, if I had a daughter I wouldn't want her to marry someone I hadn't met. They didn't speak a word of English and we didn't speak a word of their language, so she had to translate everything. Her dad would talk for about five minutes, so I would ask her what he said, and she would just say "oh nothing."

Much of the time I had to communicate with them using scuba diving hand signals. We had discussed her dad's father of the bride speech many times, and I was told that he knew what he was going to say. On our actual wedding day, when it came to that moment, she told him to stand up, I could see that he hadn't a clue what was going on, so I just said to my wife to tell her dad to say thank you and sit down, which he did. She spent most of our wedding reception evening in her parents' bedroom with them, I had to track her down so that we could have our first dance. Which did feel kind of confusing, though I just figured it was because her parents were much older and needed assistance due to language barriers.

The first year of our marriage wasn't too bad although it had its challenges as the visa rules prevented her from being able to work or have any kind of income. Everything I suggested that she do to get out of the house and make friends or even just to occupy her time and mind, she dismissed as a bad idea. I was still working nights which felt like it was causing a little tension between us, so I changed jobs so that I could work days and we could see each other more. That change also created tension between us as I was earning less money every month, although I still earned enough to cover our living expenses. It started with comments from her about how I wasn't successful enough and I wasn't earning enough, then she would go on to criticise how I would do the housework and wasn't doing it properly. She suggested that I should get a shed, so I could get changed in there when I came home from work as she felt my work clothes smelled of diesel. There were all sorts of other negative remarks as to why I wasn't a good enough husband and she compared me to her friends husbands. Each comment on its own wasn't too detrimental but the build-up over time was really hurtful and knocked my self-esteem.

The second-year things started to change, her mum's health was starting to fade so I said she could go over and spend some time with her mum. She went over for three months, and I joined her for the last two weeks. When I went out, I had to meet her sister for the first time at the airport, then her sister took me to where my wife was for dinner. After dinner we had numerous taxis to meet up with their cousins who took us to sleep at their house for a few hours before we embarked on a long car journey to the city where my wife's parents lived. The following day after about 6 hours of driving and various phone calls to keep them updated on their mum's condition, there were some deafening screeches from the back of the car. Their mum had passed away with still an hour's drive to go. Once we got there I realised just how different our cultures were. When a loved one passed no one was allowed to sleep until the deceased had been buried, that happened two days later, just what I wanted to hear after only three hours sleep in the last 27 hours! It was exhausting. After all of the funeral proceedings were done we left her family and went our own way, with a few days in another city before flying home together. I had missed her but not her negative comments, which now started getting worse as she saw it as my fault that she didn't get to spend enough time with her mum or to see her that last time. I felt like this was pretty unfair, as it was her parents' decision to have their children raised by a nanny and her decision to leave home for study and travel as well as choosing to marry a man from another country, it really felt like she didn't want to take responsibility for her own decisions and needed someone else to blame.

The next year her comments got worse and worse, as did the way I felt about myself, she had an amazing ability to flip things over and make me feel like the results of her decisions and actions were somehow my fault. She told me that her cousins had had twins by IVF and asked how I felt about doing the same so she only had to get pregnant once, I refused point blank. I didn't believe in it, unless we had been trying to get her pregnant for a few years with no success then it could be an option but not when we hadn't tried. She went to her country again for another three months, I went for the first two weeks then left her there. While we were there she suggested getting sexual health tests done, initially I thought I'd prefer to get them done at home but then as I hadn't ever had one, thought it may not be a bad thing. She wanted to make sure everything was ok with both of us before she tried to get pregnant. I thought maybe if we had children she would be happier and not give me such a hard time. I had started my own business outside of my full-time job to increase my income and was working towards being in that business full time. She was also working full time, as she now had permission to remain and work most of the time away from home, I had suspicions of some of the stories she told me about her work but with no proof I didn't say too much.

This being the fourth year of our marriage she had another trip to her home country, I didn't go on this trip as I had too much on with work and business. Though secretly I just wanted the peace and quiet. The day before she left we had unprotected sex which was the first time in our marriage. About a month after she had left she told me she was pregnant, just like that? First time? Wow!

When we were talking a month later she revealed to me that the baby had no heart rate and the doctors recommended that the pregnancy be terminated. She decided that was best and said that it had been done the day before. I didn't really know how to process my feelings or even what the feelings were, it just felt like someone had ripped my insides out. I did my best to support her though, I didn't really know what I could do for her, being so far away. The following two-weeks I felt like things couldn't possibly get worse, I got taken by surprise to say the least. To start with, I was told that she was sick and that it would have been passed onto me, so I needed to go to the doctor. I enquired to what my doctor would need to test for, she said she had syphilis. That really didn't sound good as I knew that I had been faithful, so I went to the local clinic the next day and had all the tests done and the results were all clear. The doctor that gave me the results confirmed that unless my wife had some kind of blood transfusion with infected blood, she had been having an affair. The only thing that seemed strange, was that they didn't check my sperm like they did at the hospital in her country the previous year.

That same week whilst searching for a flash drive that I had mislaid I found one of her note books. It was all written in her language, which I didn't understand aside from a few things such as, hotel names, men's names and prices. Along with that were hundreds of condoms, different to the ones we had been using, newspaper clippings of massage parlour adverts, bank statements in her name showing deposits of hundreds of pounds around three different cities, hundreds of miles away from the place she had informed me she was working as a waitress. I got her little book translated, in a way I was hoping that it wasn't what I was suspecting but the translation just made me feel worse as not only did it confirm my suspicions, it was also very explicit. My heart just sank to the ground and filled me with thousands of unanswered questions. How could she do this to me? Why would she do this? How could this be going on without me knowing? Why couldn't she talk to me? What do I do now? How can I talk to anyone about this?

They went on and on with no real answers! I felt so much shame for myself and the situation I was in. I felt that somehow, I had failed, even if I didn't know how, where or when, and that ending our marriage would be the best thing now.

I really didn't know how to bring this up either on text message or voice calls, so I just kept communication to a minimum. I spoke to a family law solicitor to see where I stood legally and told my family we were going through some challenging times, which they had suspected anyway, I just didn't mention any real details.

I followed the advice of the solicitor as I didn't really know how to handle this for myself or who I could really talk to without being criticised or judged, the solicitor said not to mention what I had found or what I was thinking of until she was back home as she may just never come back which would make divorce or moving on very difficult. I had the day off work to collect her from the airport and planned to get things out in the open that day, I didn't feel comfortable talking about it all in the car, so I waited until we got home. I'm sure the atmosphere was so tight it could be cut with a rusty butter knife. When we got home I said that we needed to talk, I told her that my test results were clear and I wanted to know where she got syphilis from. She tried to tell me she must have gotten it from a towel or a toilet seat which I refused to believe. She couldn't give me an answer, so I moved on to all of the other stuff. The condoms; she was looking after for a friend who had now left the country. That reminded me of high-school when friends got caught with cigarettes, they would get another friend to phone their parents and say they were theirs instead. All her explanations just seemed made up and crazy, I just couldn't believe them, probably not helped by me no longer trusting anything that she said. After a while she just said that it's better that she didn't talk – how do we move forward if we don't talk? I didn't feel I had any options left, I threatened her with divorce if she didn't tell me the truth. I went out for a walk and when I came back I said that I needed the truth even if she felt I wouldn't like it. She still refused to talk so I got the divorce papers served. I felt kind of bad doing this the day she got back but things would only have gotten worse and worse if I left it any longer.

The next day I got home to find her in tears, her having read the divorce papers and reality was setting in, she knew I wasn't messing around. She said that she had spoken with some of her friends and they recommended that she tell me the truth. She said she had been working in a friend's office taking calls from the working girls and taking notes for the boss. She didn't feel she could tell me as she didn't think my family would approve. The money she had lent to a friend who was paying her back bit by bit, wherever she was, when she got the money. She still couldn't explain the syphilis or the condoms, then she said she was never even pregnant while she was away. The hospital we went to in her country was an IVF clinic, she wanted me to think I had got her pregnant naturally before she went then get herself pregnant with a multiple birth from the clinic instead. That completely destroyed any chance of me trusting her again, I also felt like I was in an impossible position. I felt I was having to choose between continuing with the divorce and with the possibility that she could come back one day with multiple children, saying these are yours and I need you to pay for them, which may cause issues with a new partner if I had moved on. And the other-side was to let her get herself pregnant, knowing there was a strong chance that our relationship still wouldn't last but knowing that if it ended and I moved on, I'd be a single dad with however many kids. This would be easier for a new partner to understand than the other option.

It was a really big decision to make from a really low place, mentally and emotionally.

I decided on the second option, I needed to have some kind of certainty in my own mind as to what she was likely to do. Two months later off she went for 2 ½ months and came back pregnant with twins. Though the pregnancy went well they had to perform an emergency C-section early as the second baby was no longer growing, though both were born healthy.

While the babies were in special care for almost three weeks, their mum only went to visit them twice! The nurses at the hospital were starting to get concerned as I was going in every day and they said that if she didn't start spending time with the babies to bond with them they would have to get social services involved. I didn't like the idea of that so the next day I took her in to see them before I went to work, leaving her there for the day. She did start to bond a little and the hospital were happy to let the children come home with us.

Four months later my neighbours informed me that it had been noticed that my wife was going out and leaving the children home alone for a few hours at a time and was I aware of it? I was not and certainly didn't agree with her doing so. I went in and talked with her and let her know that she had been seeing doing it and that it must never happen again. She just said that they were her kids and she would raise them how she wants. I replied, saying that she may raise them how she wants as long as they're not being put at risk and that she stays within the laws of this country. If she was caught leaving them again, social services would be informed, and they had the power to take our children off of us if they felt it best for their wellbeing. Just a month later I came home from work to find that she was out, I was initially relieved to find she had taken the children with her this time. I didn't know where they were, as I walked round the house I noticed other things weren't there either, the laptop, baby swings, milk bottles, steriliser. I called her, but there was no answer, I called the two friends of hers that I actually knew but they knew nothing either. The neighbours said they saw her load the car up with the kids screaming in the back and she just put as much stuff in the car as she could, but they didn't know where she went. I called the police and reported them missing and said that I wasn't sure about her mental health at this time as I had been told she was leaving our children – just six months old at the time – home alone. They said they would look into it, and after half an hour and the police said they were aware of their location – they were safe and well. They wouldn't say where she was, only that I needed legal advice. I did speak to the solicitor but there wasn't much they could do at that time other than hire a private investigator.

Two weeks later she called me and said she did what she did to teach me a lesson. She wouldn't tell me where they were or when I could see the kids and just laughed at me. I couldn't see anything funny at all, I felt like my blood was boiling inside. After a while she agreed to bring our children over to meet me in town, when we met she said it was better to live separately as we would get more money off of the government that way, and that she didn't want any money off me, they were her kids and she would take care of them on her own. Then I started getting calls off the CSA saying that I had not been paying her any maintenance. I agreed to pay what I could afford but it was never enough for her as she believed I could afford more with a full-time job and part time business, despite being shown all bank statements and accounts. The following month, my monthly salary went out within 24 hours on legal fees and child maintenance. Out of frustration and determination I left my full-time job to focus on my business.

Things went well for a few months, then the reality of my situation hit, I was struggling financially, I really felt like I had failed as a husband, father and failing as a business owner. Kneeling on my living room floor crying, really not knowing which way to turn and contemplating running away to start again in New Zealand. The lyrics of the music I was listening too made me really stop and think, I felt like I'd been hit by a train. The lyrics from the Mike Tramp song "Better Off" resonated deeply and I felt like he was singing about my kids in the future if I didn't make some changes in my life, and no one else could do it for me, I just had no idea how!! The following week I had a meeting scheduled with a lady who was a coach. A friend of mine had a feeling she could help.

As we talked I knew I had to hire her for myself, I couldn't really afford her fees, but I also knew I couldn't afford to fail my children.

Working with my coach, I found that I had been burying and suppressing emotions for many years, and only seeing the things in my life that I didn't like or were not the way I wanted them to be. I learned some tools so that I could feel them and let them go so that they didn't consume me. One of the biggest lessons I learned was that life was happening for me instead of to me. The day my ex-wife left, although it was painful at the time, I now see as one of the greatest gifts. I didn't quit and I didn't fail, I gave it everything I could with the knowledge I had at the time. She set me free, to be able to be with someone who desires to be with me as much as I desire to be with them and loves me for who I am. I learned that a lot of the things I believed about myself were incorrect as there were two versions of me living within me; which are my natural-self and my egoic-self. My egoic-self is the version of me that wants to remain small and safe, instead of letting me grow, learn and do new things. My egoic-self looks for the world to change to match the way it believes it should be. My natural-self has more courage and faith instead of looking outside of me where I have little to no control whatsoever, it looks within me, to see what I can change, whether it is what I am thinking about a situation or what I can personally do to improve things.

One of the questions my coach asked me was, "what did I do to contribute to the situation?" My egoic-self answered first and said nothing, she did all of this to me, however my natural-self went deep within, having learned a lot more about myself and people as part of the coaching program. My natural-self said I tried to give her what she said she wanted but I would not stand up for myself until I was backed into a corner. I did not give her what she needed, I didn't even ask what her needs were as they're not always the same as what is wanted. I didn't know how to say no, so I would just say yes dear and do what I wanted. I didn't communicate how I felt or what I needed within our relationship - how could I blame her for not meeting the needs I didn't tell her about?

I found that living in the present moment is far more pleasurable that being stuck in the past or dreaming of the future. I realised that not being in the present moment I was missing out on many amazing things in my life. Looking back, I have no idea how I felt when I held my children for the first time as I wasn't present at the time, I was dreaming of a different life. I do however remember how it felt when they were older, after being coached, picking them up from nursery school and they both dropped whatever they were playing with and ran to me and clung on to a leg, each screaming daddy, daddy, daddy! Every time this happened I was just in awe of the moment, almost blessed in some way and felt like I was someone really special to them and all the things that had gone on between myself and their mum didn't matter to them it was just that moment in time.

After a few months of coaching I wrote a relationship vision, a vision of how I would like my relationship to be, what was important to me personally and within a relationship, as I learned more about myself. I tweaked it a little until it truly felt right. I have talked about this vision with some of the women I have dated since and some have said things like, "well this is ok but it's just not for me." Which I found really useful as we really wanted different things and we remained friends and moved on. The lady I am getting to know now saw it recently and asked when I wrote it as she felt it really described her and the kind of relationship she desires.

Now I have a great relationship with both of my children who both look forward to spending every weekend with their daddy. Coaching made such an impact on my life, I decided to become a coach myself and specialise in intimate relationships. I am writing a book which will be my full story, which will be more in-depth with rebuilding myself after the divorce and the journey of growth, along with some of the things I believed as a young boy and teen that had a big impact on me in the world of relationships. This book at present is going to be called The Boy With No Voice or Finding My Voice

To learn more please find me on Facebook - www.facebook.com/OfficialLoveEngineer or email: alan@love-engineers.win

45955069R00109

Made in the USA
Lexington, KY
20 July 2019